Histories and Historians *of* Hispanic America

BY

A. CURTIS WILGUS, Ph.D.

I0895946

Routledge
Taylor & Francis Group
LONDON AND NEW YORK

First published 1965 by
Frank cass

Published 2006 by Routledge
2 Park Square, Milton Park, Abingdon, Oxfordshire OX14 4RN
711 Third Avenue, New York, NY 10017

First issued in paperback 2014

Routledge is an imprint of the Taylor and Francis Group, an informa business

British Library Cataloguing in Publication Data
A catalogue record for this book is available from the British Library

Library of Congress Catalog Card Number: 65-21912

ISBN 13: 978-0-7146-2035-0 (hbk)
ISBN 13: 978-1-138-01109-0 (pbk)

LIBRARY OF LATIN AMERICAN
HISTORY AND CULTURE

GENERAL EDITOR:
DR. A. CURTIS WILGUS

INTRODUCTION TO THE FIRST EDITION

The bibliography of Hispanic America is extremely vast and remarkably varied so that whoever essays the compilation of an exhaustive bibliography of published materials on any phase of Hispanic American life must have not only abundant time at his disposal but considerable funds in order to accomplish it. Indeed, it is becoming more and more evident that the production of an exhaustive bibliography in any field and on almost any subject requires the coöperation of numerous experts. The Medina type of individual must now be replaced by a coöperating group of individual specialists. But whether the bibliographer works by himself or with others, his task is never finished and the results of his work are never satisfactory to everyone, particularly if the list is selective, for somewhere someone will find an important work (probably his own) omitted. Hence, in the preparation of this list of histories and historians—and both terms are used broadly—concerning Hispanic America, the writer would be foolhardy to lay claim to completeness; he has attempted, and attempted only, to call attention to some of the leading writers and to some of the outstanding references which deal with the subject. The classification chosen is chronological by centuries, like that in the author's *Histories of Hispanic America* (The Pan American Union, Washington, 1932) and in the Appendices, pages 573-662, in *Colonial Hispanic America* (The George Washington University Press, Washington, 1936), upon which this study is based, while the arrangement within these divisions is generally both logical and chronological. The table of contents and index have been arranged to provide a ready reference to subjects and to authors. Whenever the years of birth and death of authors have been known these have been given in connection with the first mention of the name, as well as in the author index. Spellings have been modernized, and the recent trend in capitalization has been followed. Limitations of space permit virtually no bio-bibliographical treatment, much as that is to be desired, nor can more than a brief mention be made of most of the items. Despite these limitations, however, it is hoped that some value will accrue, especially to the graduate student of Hispanic American history and civilization, from this mere mention of selected authors and their works.

The writer wishes to record here his grateful appreciation for the assistance rendered him by Dr. James Alexander Robertson, Dr. Philip Ainsworth Means, Dr. Raul d'Eça, Mr. Ernest Kletsch, Miss Carmen Sullivan, the Library staff of the Pan American Union, and the Inter-American Bibliographical and Library Association, under the auspices of which this work is published. Two persons have rendered invaluable assistance: Miss Catherine Phelps, the writer's secretary, whose painstaking aid has been of inestimable value; and Dr. C. K. Jones, whose advice, assistance, and encouragement have been a constant source of inspiration.

A. CURTIS WILGUS.

Washington, D. C.,
April 2, 1936.

INTRODUCTION TO THE SECOND EDITION

Since the publication of the first edition of this volume six years ago, many important works dealing with Hispanic America have appeared and considerable new interest in the field has been manifest both by the public and by students. Consequently it has seemed desirable to issue the work in a revised, corrected, and augmented form. It is hoped that individuals interested in the subject may find this edition even more useful than the previous one.

A. CURTIS WILGUS.

April 2, 1942

INTRODUCTION TO REPRINT EDITION

A book becomes scarce for many reasons: it has a paper binding and disintegrates; it is a popular text and the edition sells rapidly; it is a valuable research tool and it disappears from library shelves; it is destroyed by fire, flood, and other Acts of God. The second edition of this volume went out-of-print for all of these reasons — hence this reprint by the Cooper Square Publishers, Inc. This organization has made a name for itself in the field of reprints, and its present project of reproducing in facsimile form classic studies in Latin American history and culture, most of them listed in this guide, should attract wide and favorable attention. The author is pleased that his book has been selected for this series.

A. CURTIS WILGUS

June, 1965

TABLE OF CONTENTS

CHAPTER ONE

SIXTEENTH CENTURY WORKS [1]

A. Introduction
B. General works
 1. History, geography, description, etc.
 2. Voyages and travels
C. Works on individual countries and regions
 1. Brazil
 2. Mexico
 3. Florida
 4. West Indies
 5. Tierra Firme
 6. Peru
 7. La Plata
 8. Chile

A. Introduction [2]

When the Iberians, after several centuries of fighting the Moslem, launched upon the conquest of America they little knew what was before them. But their religious zeal and their desire for gold and glory overcame all obstacles, and during the sixteenth century they conquered or claimed more than two-thirds of the Western Hemisphere. The mechanical process of conquering two continents resulted inevitably in the recording of experiences, in speculation concerning the land and its people who were found in a state of nature, in letters, memoirs, reports, and in relations, histories, etc.

B. General Works

1. *History, Geography, Description, etc.*

Among the earliest and most frequently quoted of the histories concerning America, or as it soon came to be called, the Indies or the New World, is that by Gonzalo Fernández de Oviedo y Valdes (1478-1557) whose *Historia general y natural de las indias* was published at Sevilla in 1535. This had been preceded by another brief work, now excessively rare, entitled *Sumario de la natural y general historia de las indias* (Toledo, 1526). The

[1] For a more detailed description of the leading sixteenth century histories and historians see my series of articles in the *Bulletin* of the Pan American Union, July, September, 1933; April, May, June, 1936; May, 1937; January, 1939; May, 1940; and March, 1941.

[2] Because of limitations of space, the compiler has attempted no extensive analysis of the general political, social, economic, religious, or intellectual conditions existing in each century. He has, however, tried in as brief a way as possible to indicate certain trends and to point out certain influences affecting historians and their works in each century.

work of 1535 containing nineteen books or parts was continued in 1557 at Valladolid when the twentieth book appeared. The entire manuscript written by Oviedo seems never to have been published in its entirety, although fifty books were printed at Madrid in four volumes 1851-55. Various abridged editions in foreign languages have been published, the first English translation appearing at London in 1555, the work of Richard Eden (ca. 1521-1576) under the title *General history of the West Indies*. Oviedo derived many of the facts for his history from direct observation since he spent twenty-four years in America, returning to Spain as a gray-haired man.

Another work frequently cited, but of indifferent value because it is based on hearsay rather than upon documents, is that by the Priest Francisco López de Gómara (1511-ca.-1560) entitled *La historia de las indias y conquista de México* published in two parts at Zaragoza in 1552. The history describes the conquests of Peru and Mexico, and its circulation was prohibited soon after publication. In 1596 the first translation in English appeared at London made by Thomas Nicholas in 1578. This, however, dealt only with the portion relating to Mexico as noted below. The newest English edition of the 1578 translation is entitled *The conquest of the West Indies* (New York, 1940). The author was never in America, and he was accused by his contemporaries of fabricating many facts. In 1932 at Madrid the first part of this work dealing with Peru appeared in two volumes.

One of the most impassioned writers of history in this century was Bartolomé de las Casas (1474-1566), the "Apostle of the Indies." His chief works, which because of their nature are not always trustworthy, are the *Brevíssima relación de la destrucción de das indias* (Sevilla, 1552); the *Historia de las indias* (6 vols., Madrid, 1875-79) taken from the original manuscript begun by Las Casas in 1520 and completed in 1561; and the *Historia apologética de las indias* (Madrid, 1867) copied by E. G. Squier (1821-1888) from the author's unpublished manuscript completed about 1550. A great number of editions of these volumes were subsequently published in foreign languages, particularly by the French and Dutch who used the books as propaganda against Spain. What appears to be the first English edition of the *Brevíssima relación* was published at London in 1583 as part of a now very rare book entitled *The Spanish colonie*, etc.

An historian of greater authority is José de Acosta (ca. 1539-1600) whose *Historia natural y moral de las indias* was published at Sevilla in 1590, although an earlier edition of books one and two had been printed in Latin in 1588 and 1589 at Salamanca. The first English edition was printed in 1604 at London while the best English edition can be found in the Hakluyt Society publications, volumes LX and LXI (original series, 1878-79). Acosta spent seventeen years in Peru as a Jesuit official, and his history is marked by religious coloring and philosophical treatment.

A work of considerable value frequently referred to is *De orbe novo* by the Italian churchman and courtier, Pietro Martire d'Anghiera (ca. 1455-1526), usually called Peter Martyr, who is generally considered the first historian of America. The first three decades of this work were published in Latin at Alcalá in 1516. The first complete edition of the eight decades to appear was that of 1530 at the same place. An excellent English edition in two volumes was edited by F. A. MacNutt (1863-1927) and published at New York in 1912. The first English edition was published at London in 1555.

Another Italian, Girolamo Benzoni (1519-ca. 1572), brought out at Venice in 1565 a superficial work, somewhat prejudicial to the Spaniards, entitled *La historia del mondo nuovo,* an English translation of which may be found in the Hakluyt Society publications, volume XXI (original series, 1857). The work has been translated into several other languages but never into Spanish. The author went to America at the age of twenty-two and stayed fourteen years collecting material for his volume. The illustrations in the book are from the author's own sketches.

A pretentious undertaking written in Italian is *Le relationi universali,* published at Venice in 1579. It constitutes a general history and description of the principal parts of the world, and the author was Giovanni Botero (1540-1617). In 1748 a Spanish edition appeared at Gerona with the title frequently encountered, namely, *Descripción de todas las provincias, reynos, estados y ciudades del mundo.* This had been translated by the churchman, Jayme Rebullosa, who has often been misnamed the author. What appears to be the first English translation was published at London in 1603.

Another type of general work is that by Juan López de Velasco, entitled *Geografía y descripción universal de las indias.* It was written probably between the years 1571 and 1574, but was not published in book form until the nineteenth century when it appeared in 1894 or 1895 at Madrid. The author compiled the volume largely from documents in Spain which were placed at his disposal by the Council of the Indies.

Another geographical work which did not appear until the nineteenth century is the *Relaciones geográficas de indias* (Lima, 1885) by Lorenzo Suárez de Figueroa. The manuscript was written in 1586.

A rare and valuable work also descriptive of America, as well as of other parts of the world, is that by Martín Fernández de Enciso (1470-1528) entitled briefly *Suma de geografía* (Sevilla, 1519). The material on America was largely written from personal knowledge.

A work of a descriptive nature concerning the west coast region of South America which seems to have been written at the end of the century is *La descripción y población de las indias,* by the Bishop and Dominican, Reginaldo de Lizárraga (ca. 1540-ca. 1612), who lived in Peru from 1555 to 1599. Two copies of this manuscript are extant, one in the library of the

University of Zaragoza and the other in the library of the University of San Marcos at Lima. The latter manuscript was hurriedly edited by Carlos A. Romero (b. 1863) and published in *Revista Histórica* at Lima in 1907. This was reprinted in book form the next year at the same place. The Zaragoza manuscript was edited by Manuel Serrano y Sanz (1868-1932), and published at Madrid in 1909. Dr. Philip Ainsworth Means (b. 1892) considers this work more informative than that by Benzoni.

Another descriptive work, valuable especially for the early history of the Peruvian and Mexican Indians, was written by the Augustinian Friar Jerónimo de Román y Zamora (ca. 1536-1597). The author never went to America, but as an adviser to Philip II he was in a position to use a great amount of documentary material. His chief work is entitled *Repúblicas del mundo . . .*, published in two volumes at Medina del Campo in 1575. The second edition (three volumes at Salamanca) contains more material on America. A new Spanish edition was published at Madrid in two volumes in 1897 under the editorship of D. L. d'Orvenipe (1865-1921). It was called *Repúblicas de indias.*

Still another descriptive work was prepared by Corneille Wytfliet under the title *Descriptionis Ptolemaicae augmentum* (Louvain, 1597). This was translated into French, probably by Giovanni Antonio Magini (1555-1617), and published as Part One of Wytfliet's *Histoire universelle des Indes occidentales* (Dovay, 1607).

In 1591 was published at Mexico City the first part of a work intended to be a treatise on universal knowledge. It was entitled *Primera parte de los problemas y secretas maravillosas de las indias.* The book lacked in scientific observation, and no further parts were published. A second edition appeared at Mexico City in 1913. The author was Juan de Cárdenas (b. 1563).

Two works of an historical nature but dealing with medicinal plants in the New World are of great value to the student of the sixteenth century. The first to appear was by Nicolás Monardes (ca. 1512-1588), entitled *Primera y segunda y tercera partes de la historia medicinal de las cosas que se traen de nuestras indias occidentales que sirven de medicina.* This was published in an incomplete edition at Sevilla in 1565. The whole work was issued at the same place in 1574 and 1580. It was published in many other languages, the first English edition being that at London in 1596, which bore the title *Joyful news out of the new found world.* Another somewhat similar work of this century, but dealing chiefly with Spanish North America, was by Francisco Hernández (ca. 1517-ca. 1587), who was sent by Philip II to study the medicinal plants of New Spain. The work, which was illustrated with some twelve hundred colored drawings of plants, bore the title *Cuatro libros de la naturaleza y virtudes de las plantas y animales de uso medicinal en la Nueva España.* It first appeared at Mexico City in 1615. In 1888 a new edition was published at Mexico City. In 1926 at the same place appeared a facsimile edition of his *De antiquitatibus Novæ Hispaniæ* treating Indian medical history to 1519. Because many of the plants which he describes appear in other parts of the Indies, his work has considerable value to the historian of the colonial epoch.

An exceedingly valuable volume describing the military organization of the Indies in the sixteenth century is Bernardo de Vargas Machuca's (1557-1622) *Milicia y descripción de las indias* published at Madrid in 1599. This was republished in a second edition at Madrid in 1892. The author served as a soldier in Italy, Spain, and America, and in 1599, at the request of the Council of the Indies, he proposed a method of pacifying the Araucanian Indians of Chile.

2. *Voyages and Travels*

A work of an entirely different nature appeared in Italian in three volumes at Venice between 1550 and 1556. It bore a long title briefly cited as *Navigationi et viaggi* and was by the historian and geographer, Giovanni Battista Ramusio (1485-1557). Volume III particularly relates almost exclusively to the New World, but its value has been debated.

A somewhat similar work was published at London in 1555 under the editorship of Richard Eden with the title *The decades of the new world or West India.* This was an adaptation of parts of Peter Martyr's eight decades with additions made by the enthusiastic editor and compiler. The work was augmented and rearranged by Richard Willes and published at London in 1577 in one large volume.

A third collection of voyages was begun by Theodore de Bry (1528-1598) under the title *Americæ sive peregrinationum in indiam occidentalem,* the first two volumes of which appeared at Frankfurt in 1590. In the following years to 1634, forty-two more volumes were printed at the same place.

A fourth collection, in imitation of that of De Bry, is the *Sammlung von sechs und zwanzig schiffahrten* by Levinus Hulsius (ca. 1546-1606), published in twenty-six volumes at Nüremberg and Frankfurt between 1598 and 1650. Only part of this work, however, deals with America.

A fifth collection describes the first French voyages to America, particularly to Florida and Brazil. The work is entitled *Les trois mondes* and was compiled by Le Seigneur de la Popellinière (1541-1608). It was published at Paris in 1582.

A sixth collection dealing largely with English explorations was compiled by Richard Hakluyt (ca. 1552-1616), entitled briefly *The principal navigations, voyages, traffiques and discoveries of the English nation.* This was published at London in three volumes from 1598 to 1600, the last volume particularly relating to America. This work had been augmented largely from his *Divers voyages touching the discovery of America and the islands adjacent* (London, 1582) and from his *The principal voyages and discoveries of the English written in the compass of 1500 years* (London, 1589).

A record of a single voyage of importance is that by the Venetian Antonio Pigafetta (1480-1534) who as an eyewitness told the story of Magellan's voyage around the world in his *Il viaggio fatto dagli Spagnuoli atorno al mondo* published in an incomplete edition at Venice probably in 1534 or 1536. An English edition appeared at London in 1555 in Richard Eden's *The decades of the new world.* The best English edition is that edited and translated by James Alexander Robertson (1873-1939) under the title *Magellan's voyage around the world* (3 vols., Cleveland, 1906).

C. Works on Individual Countries and Regions

Among the works of the sixteenth century are a number which deal particularly with geographical regions. It is obviously impossible to mention all such references and in consequence only those of greatest value or interest are here cited.

1. *Brazil*

Three sixteenth century general works dealing exclusively with Brazil are usually considered of importance largely because there are no others of great merit. The first is by Pedro de Magalhães de Gandavo (b. 1540), who aimed to stimulate migration to Brazil, and is entitled *Historia da provincia de Santa Cruz.* It was published at Lisbon in 1576, and is the first general history of Brazil. An English translation in two volumes under the title *The histories of Brazil* was printed at New York by the Cortes Society in 1912. The second work bears the title *Tratado descriptivo do Brasil* and was written by Gabriel Soares de Souza in 1587 but it was not published in an accurate edition until 1851, when, under the editorship of Francisco Adolpho de Varnhagen (1816-1878), it appeared at Rio de Janeiro. The third work, written by Fernão Cardim (d. 1625) in three parts at the end of the sixteenth century, is descriptive of the country, the natives, and the Jesuit missions. It appeared finally in print at Rio de Janeiro in 1925 under the title *Tratados da terra e gente do Brasil.*

A work of considerable value for its description of the Indians of eastern Brazil was written by Hans Staden (ca. 1520-ca. 1557), who went to Brazil in 1547. Two years later his vessel was wrecked off São Vicente and Staden was captured by the Indians, with whom he remained until 1555. His story was told in his *Warachtige historie,* published first at Marburg in 1557. An English edition was published by the Hakluyt Society at London in 1874 as Volume LI, first series.

A second valuable autobiographical account is that by Alvar Núñez Cabeza de Vaca (ca. 1490-1564), famed in North America as a walker, who wrote, after his experiences in Brazil and Paraguay, *La relación y comentarios . . .*, which was published in one volume at Valladolid in 1555. In 1891 the Hakluyt Society published at London an English translation as part two of Volume LXXXI of its first series.

Another work which deals in part with Brazil was begun by João de Barros (1496-1570) and continued into the next century by Diogo do Couto (1542-1616). It bore various titles but it is usually cited as *Da Asia.* It was divided into decades, the first being published in one volume at Lisbon in 1552. This was followed by the second decade in a second volume published the next year also at Lisbon. The third decade appeared at the same place in 1563. The fourth decade did not appear until it was published at Madrid in 1615. The work was finally completed in twenty-four volumes; the best edition, and the first complete one, was published at Lisbon between 1778 and 1788. This work constitutes the best account of the early Portuguese discoveries in existence and treats of the Portuguese discovery and conquest of Brazil very thoroughly. The whole work is based upon archival materials.

A lesser work of Portuguese explorations appeared at Lisbon in 1563 under the title *Tratado que compôs o nobre e notavel capitão Antonio Galvão. . . .* This appeared in an English edition at London in 1601 corrected and published by Richard Hakluyt under the title *The discoveries of the world from the first original unto the year 1555, by Antonie Galvano.* The Hakluyt Society issued the work at London in 1862 as volume XXX, first series.

2. *Mexico*

A number of notable works concerning Mexico or New Spain were written in this century, although several did not appear until later centuries. Among the latter are the *Historia eclesiástica indiana* by Fray Gerónimo de Mendieta (d. 1604) which did not appear until it was published at Mexico City in 1870; the excellent, widely known, and frequently printed *Historia verdadera de la conquista de la Nueva España* by Bernal Díaz del Castillo (1492-1581) which appeared in a corrupt form at Madrid in 1632, but which was published in a much more accurate Spanish edition of two volumes at Mexico City (1904-05) under the editorship of Genaro García (1867-1920), and in an excellent five-volume English edition under the editorship of A. P. Maudslay (b. 1850) by the Hakluyt Society (1908-16) as Volumes XXIII-XXV, XXX, XL (second series); the brief 41 page *Relación sobre la conquista de México* by Andrés de Tapia (ca. 1495-ca. 1539) published by Joaquín García Icazbalceta (1825-1894) in volume II, pages 554 ff. of his *Colección de documentos para la historia de México* (2 vols., Mexico, 1858-66); the *Sumaria relación de las cosas de la Nueva España,* containing among other information an account of the descendents of the conquerors and early inhabitants of New Spain, written probably about the end of the sixteenth century by Baltasar Dorantes de Carranza (ca. 1550-ca. 1604) but not printed until 1902 at Mexico City; and the long lost *Crónica de la Nueva España* by Francisco Cervantes de Salazar (ca. 1514-1575) begun in 1560 but not published until it began to appear at Madrid in 1914.

In this century was written the extremely valuable *Historia general de las cosas de Nueva España* by Bernardino de Sahagún (ca. 1500-1590), the first eleven books of which appeared in three volumes at Mexico City in 1829 and 1830, and the twelfth book of which appeared finally at Mexico City in 1840 under the title *La aparición de Nuestra Señora de Guadelupe,* an English translation of which was made by Fanny Bandelier entitled *A history of ancient Mexico* (Nashville, 1932). Sahagún's work was printed in England in Kingsborough's *Antiquities of Mexico* (9 vols., London, 1830-48). Volume VII (pages 1-464) contained the whole twelve books of his general history, except Book Six, chapters 1-40, which are to be found in volume V (pages 345-493). The general history was reprinted at Mexico City in five volumes in 1938.

Other works are the account of Hernando Cortés (1485-1547) contained in his five letters which have appeared in several languages in many editions, one of the best English editions being *The letters of Cortés* edited by F. A. MacNutt (2 vols., New York and London, 1908); the *Noticias históricas de la Nueva España* by Juan Suárez de Peralta (b. 1536) dealing with Mexico from the earliest times to the period of Drake, but not published until 1878 at Madrid; the *Historia de los indios de Nueva España y islas de Tierra Firme*—including the life of Montezuma—(2 vols. and Atlas, Mexico, 1867-80) by the Dominican Diego Durán (ca. 1538-ca. 1588); the *Relación breve y verdadera de algunas cosas . . . que sucedieron al padre Alonso Ponce en las provincias de Nueva España* (2 vols., Madrid, 1873) dealing not only with Mexico but with Cuba and parts of present-day Central America, and written about the Franciscans probably by the spiritual brothers, Alonso de Ciudad-Real (1551-1617) and Alonso de San Juan; and the *Historia de la Nueva España* by Fray Francisco de Aguilar, called Alonso de Aguilar, a companion of Cortés, which was first published by Luis González Obregón in volume VII of the *Anales del Museo Nacional,* but finally printed in a revised edition by Alfonso Teja Zabre (Mexico, 1938).

An excellent picture of the advance of the Mexican frontier to 1584, as well as an interpretation of the significance of the frontier, was written by Baltasar de Obregón (b. 1544). It is entitled *Historia de los descubrimientos antiguos y modernos de la Nueva España.* It was written in 1584 but was not published until it appeared at Mexico City in 1924. An English translation was made by George Peter Hammond (b. 1896) and Agapito Rey and was published at Los Angeles in 1928.

A sixteenth century account of the Indians of Mexico bore the title *Historia de los indios de Nueva España.* It was written by Toribio de Benavente Motolinía (d. ca. 1568), as he is usually called. It first appeared at Barcelona in 1858 as volume I of Joaquín García Icazbalceta's *Colección de documentos para la historia de México.* Another interesting work which throws light on the Indians of New Spain was written by Fray Juan Baptista who compiled instructions for confessing the Indians and who included in his book many papal bulls concerning church affairs. His volume is entitled *Advertencias para los confessores de los naturales* (2 vols., Mexico, 1600).

Two volumes, both written and published in this century, should be noted. In 1596 at Madrid was printed the first part of Agustín Dávila Padilla's (1562-1604) *Historia de la fundación y discurso de la provincia de Santiago de México* which constitutes a valuable account written from the documents of the earliest missions in America. The second part of this work was completed by Alonso Franco y Ortega (b. 1616) in 1645 but it was not published until 1900. In 1554 Gómara published his *Historia de México* at Antwerp, which was in reality a reprint of the second part of his general history. This was translated into English by Thomas Nicholas and printed for the first time at London in 1578 under the title *The pleasant history of the conquest of the West India.*

A volume of poetry in 20 cantos, on which the author worked seven years to collect the facts, was published at Madrid in 1599 under the title *El peregrino indiano.* It dealt with the years 1519 to 1540 and told the story of the conquest of Mexico. The author was Antonio de Saavedra Guzmán, a *corregidor* at Zacatecas, and his work was the first printed about Mexico by a person born there. Prescott made use of it in his history. In 1840 an edition was published at Madrid.

The story of the early civilizations of Yucatan and Central America is told by Diego de Landa (1524-1579), a Spaniard who became a Franciscan in 1541. He reached Yucatan in 1549 and zealously destroyed Maya books and images although he paradoxically saved much valuable information about the Indians for posterity. He probably compiled his book at the monastery of San Francisco at Guadalajara. The entire manuscript has never been found, but in 1864 the Abbé Brasseur de Bourbourg found a condensation which he published at Paris the same year under the title *Relation des choses de Yucatan.* A work of the same title with the text in Spanish and French was published at Paris in two volumes, 1928-29. The first English edition, and a most excellent one, limited to fifty copies and hand colored, was published by the Maya Society (Baltimore, 1937) under the title *Yucatan before and after the conquest.* This was edited and translated by William Gates (1864-1940). A second English edition was made by Alfred M. Tozzer (b. 1877) based on the text by C. P. Bowditch and was published at Cambridge, Mass. in 1941. A good Spanish edition was printed at Mérida in Yucatan and in Mexico City in 1938.

3. *Florida*

Several valuable works deal with Florida in this century. The first is *La relación y comentarios* of Alvar Núñez Cabeza de Vaca, already mentioned, which was first published in 1555 at Valladolid, describing personal adventures in Florida and parts of New Spain and South America. The part of the *Relación* dealing with regions in New Spain, however, was first published in 1542 at Zamora under the title *Naufragios* . . . and there are now only two known copies in existence. The best English edition of the North American adventures are by Buckingham Smith (1810-1871), published in 1851 (and a better edition of 1873), and by Fanny Bandelier (1905). The second work to appear dealt with Soto in Florida. It was written in Portuguese and briefly entitled *Relação verdadeira.* The author is known only as the "Gentleman of Elvas" and the book was printed first at Evora in 1557. The first English translation was made by Richard Hakluyt and was published at London in 1609 under the caption *Virginia richly valued,* which in 1611 was changed to a more appropriate title. The most recent and best English edition is that by James Alexander Robertson (New Haven, 1932-33), published in two volumes with a facsimile of the original manuscript. The third work is laudatory, frequently fanciful, and not entirely trustworthy. It is by the Inca Garcilaso de la Vega (1539-1616) and bears the title *La Florida del Inca.* It was completed perhaps in 1591 but was first published at Lisbon in 1605 and records the adventures of Hernando de Soto as seen mainly by an eyewitness who gave the story to Garcilaso.

A fourth account of the Spaniards in Florida is by Gonzalo Solís de Merás, a companion of Pedro Menéndez. It is entitled *Pedro Menéndez de Avilés . . . memorial* and it first appeared in *La Florida; su conquista y colonización por Pedro Menéndez de Avilés* (2 vols., Madrid, 1893) by Eugenio Ruidíaz y Caravia. Mrs. Jeannette Thurber Connor translated it into English and published it through the Florida State Historical Society at Deland in 1923.

A fifth account deals with the French in Florida. It was written by Jean Ribaut (ca.1520-1565) and appeared in French and in English at London in 1563. The French title was *Histoire de l'expedition française en Florida* and the English title was *The whole and true discovery of Terra Florida.* The work has been reprinted many times, one of the best being a facsimile reprint of the English edition just mentioned which Mrs. Connor issued at Deland in 1927 through the Florida State Historical Society.

A sixth and rare account, dealing with the French in Florida, is *L'Histoire notable de la Florida* . . . (Paris, 1586) by René Goulain de Laudonnière which dealt with four French expeditions to the region in 1562, 1564, 1565, and 1567. An English translation is entitled *History of the first attempt of the French to colonize . . . Florida.* It was printed in *Historical collections of Louisiana and Florida* (New York, 1869, New Series, pp. 165-362) edited by Benjamin Franklin French (1799-1877).

A seventh work dealing with Florida in this century is entitled *Documents relating to the expedition of Don Tristán de Luna y Orellana for the conquest of La Florida in 1559-1561* edited by Herbert I. Priestley (b. 1875) for the Florida State Historical Society and published in two volumes at Deland in 1928.

4. *West Indies*

A curious volume dealing with the discovery of the West Indies and neighboring regions was written in 1524 by a friend of Columbus, Alexander Geraldinus (ca. 1455-1525). This account, however, was not published until it appeared in Latin at Rome in 1631 briefly entitled *Itinerarium ad regiones sub æquinoctiali.* The author as papal legate of Alexander VI traveled widely, and his work is in consequence very valuable because he came into intimate contact with many of the early discoverers.

5. *Tierra Firme*

Another region frequently treated by Spanish histories of this century is Tierra Firme. It was in this period that Pascual de Andagoya (ca. 1495-1548) wrote his complaining and inaccurate *Relación de sucesos de Pedrarias Dávila en las provincias de tierra firme* which, however, was not published until the nineteenth century, the first Spanish edition appearing at Madrid in 1829. The best English edition is by Sir Clements R. Markham (1830-1916), published in 1865 by the Hakluyt Society as Volume XXXIV (original series). Another work not printed until later is that by Pedro de Aguado. About 1581 he wrote a manuscript which was first published in three volumes at Bogotá in 1906 under the title *Recopilación historial.* This appeared in a new edition of two volumes at Madrid in 1916 and 1917 under the title *Historia de Santa Marta y nuevo reino de Granada,* and in a three-volume edition at the same place in 1930. A second manuscript by the same author, completed in the sixteenth century, was published at Caracas in two volumes (1913-15) under the title *Historia de Venezuela.* A new edition of this work appeared at Madrid in two volumes in 1918 and 1919.

A well known English work describing a portion of this region, and especially beliefs about the Southern Mysteries and El Dorado in particular, is *The discovery of the large, rich, and beautiful empire of Guiana* by Sir Walter Raleigh (ca. 1552-1618). This account is based on his second voyage (1595) and was published at London in 1596. A recent edition of the work appeared at the same place in 1928. The Hakluyt Society published an edition at London in 1848 (first series, volume III).

A work of entirely different nature and of considerably less value than the works just mentioned is a heroic poem containing some 150,000 lines.

It is entitled *Elegías de varones ilustres de indias* and the author was Juan de Castellanos (1523-1605) who spent much of his life in compiling biographies of the early *Conquistadores* and then turning their stories into verse. The work is in four parts, the first of which appeared at Madrid in 1589, while parts two and three appeared first at Madrid in 1850, and part four appeared first in 1886 at Madrid in two volumes under the title *Historia del nuevo reino de Granada.* The whole work deals with the conquest and settlement of the Caribbean area.

6. *Peru*

Peru was treated by several authors of the sixteenth century. Among the chief was Agustín de Zárate (ca. 1492-1560) whose *Historia del descubrimiento y conquista de la provincia del Perú* was published at Antwerp in 1555. The first edition printed in Spain appeared at Sevilla in 1577. Perhaps the best Spanish edition appeared at Madrid in 1853 edited by Enrique de Vedia. An English translation may be found in Robert Kerr's (1755-1813) *A general history and collection of voyages* (Edinburgh, 1824). The author went to Peru in 1543 as a royal official and became embroiled in the civil wars there. Upon his return to Spain, probably in 1545, he wrote these volumes from his notes made in America.

A second very valuable history of the conquest was written by a secretary of Pizarro, Francisco de Xeres (b. 1504), under the title *Verdadera relación de la conquista del Perú,* published at Sevilla in 1534. An Italian translation was published in 1535 at Venice. The best English edition was published by the Hakluyt Society at London in 1872 (Vol. XLVII, original series). The history was written in Peru at the request of Pizarro and can be considered virtually the official published record of the conquest.

Another work by a secretary of Pizarro, Pedro Sancho (d. 1547), was written in manuscript and lost, but not until Ramusio had made an Italian translation which he published in his previously mentioned *Navigationi et viaggi* at Venice in 1556. A Spanish translation was made from this by Joaquín García Icazbalceta and published in 1849 as an appendix to the Spanish edition of Prescott's *History of the conquest of Peru.* The work has appeared elsewhere, but this particular account was translated into English by Philip Ainsworth Means and published by the Cortes Society at New York in 1917 under the title *An account of the conquest of Peru.*

Still another record of the conquest is by the cousin of Francisco Pizarro, Pedro Pizarro (ca. 1515-1571). His manuscript, *Relación del descubrimiento y conquista del Perú,* is doubtless the most careful and authentic account of the activities of the Conqueror of Peru. The work itself, completed in 1571, has never been entirely published, but a part of it appeared in 1844 in volume V of the *Colección de documentos inéditos para la historia de España.* William H. Prescott (1796-1859) used the manuscript to prepare his *History of the conquest of Peru.* The work has been edited by Philip Ainsworth Means and printed in English by the Cortes Society (2 vols., New York, 1921).

Another important descriptive work dealing with Peru, particularly valuable for Inca culture, is by Pedro de Cieza de León (1518-ca. 1560). It is entitled *La crónica del Perú* and was written in four parts, the first only being published at Sevilla in 1553. The first English edition was printed at London in 1709 under the title *The seventeen years travels of Peter de Cieza.* A fair English translation of parts one, two, and four of this work appeared in the Hakluyt Society publications, volumes XXXIII and LXVIII, second part, original series (1864 and 1883) and in volumes XXXI, XLII, and LIV, second series (1913, 1918, and 1923). Part three has never been found. The author lived in Peru for sixteen years, beginning his history at Popayán in 1541 and completing it at Lima in 1550. It is interestingly written and is based largely upon observation.

A valuable work dealing with Peru, of which the first part appeared at Lisbon in 1609, is briefly entitled *Comentarios reales de los Incas.* The author was one of the foremost Peruvian chroniclers, the Inca Garcilaso de la Vega. In 1617 at Córdoba appeared the second part of the *Comentarios* under the title *Historia general del Perú.* Both of these works were written from Inca records and certain Spanish chronicles, particularly the *Historia del Perú* (now lost) by the Jesuit Blas Valera (ca. 1551-1597), of which Garcilaso had a fragment of the manuscript. These works by Garcilaso have been considered by some scholars as excellent authority for the early history of the country. The first English translation of the *Comentarios reales* was published at London in 1688 in two volumes under the title the *Royal commentaries of Peru.* The best English edition was published by the Hakluyt Society as volumes XLI and XLV (original series) in 1869 and 1871. The first part of the work gives an account of Inca history and civilization while the second part is the story of the Spanish conquest of Peru.

Another work dealing with Inca affairs is entitled *Suma y narración de los Incas.* The author was Juan de Betanzos (1510-1576), who came to Peru with Pizarro and married a daughter of Atahualpa. With the knowledge of the Quichua language he became official interpreter to the viceregal government, and Antonio de Mendoza ordered him to compile the history of the Incas, which was completed in 1551. The book was written from the native standpoint, and with considerable accuracy. The first two chapters of the manuscript were copied by Friar Gregorio de García (ca. 1560-1627) in his *Origen de los indios* (Valencia, 1607), but the complete manuscript seems never to have appeared in print, although a portion was edited by Marcos Jiménez de la Espada (1831-1898) and published at Madrid in 1880.

Between 1583 and 1613 the Indian, Felipe Huaman Poma de Ayala wrote his *Nueva corónica y buen gobierno.* This work of 1179 pages containing hundreds of illustrations was discovered by Dr. Pietschmann, librarian of the University of Göttingen, in the Royal Library at Copenhagen in 1908. The work is chiefly valuable for its illustrations of contemporary life and customs. The manuscript was published at Paris in 1936.

A work of considerable reputation but in reality an inaccurate and prejudiced account of the Peruvian Incas is found in the manuscript entitled the *Segunda parte de la historia general llamada índica* by the famed seaman, Pedro Sarmiento de Gamboa (1532-ca. 1582). This work was written in Peru in 1571 and 1572 but it was not published until it appeared in Spanish at Berlin in 1906 under the German title *Geschichte des inkareiches* with a German introduction. The next year the first English edition was published at London by the Hakluyt Society as volume XXII (second series). The first and third parts to this work were apparently never written.

A valuable but diffuse work, written probably near the end of the century, but not published in complete form until the twentieth century, was by Pedro Gutiérrez de Santa Clara (ca. 1520-ca. 1603). It finally appeared in six volumes at Madrid between 1904 and 1929 and bore the title *Historia de las guerras civiles del Perú y de otros sucesos de las indias.* José Toribio Medina (1852-1930) had earlier published a fragment in volume XXVII (Santiago, 1901) of his *Colección de historiadores de Chile.*

A brief work dealing with conditions in Peru from 1522 to 1548 appeared at Sevilla in 1549 under the long title *Verdadera relación de lo sussedido en los reynos e provincias del Perú desde la yda a ellos del virey Blasco Nuñez Vela hasta el desbarato y muerta de Gonçalo Piçarro.* The author was Nicholás de Albenino (b.ca. 1514). A French facsimile edition appeared at Paris in 1930 and an English facsimile edition was printed at Boston the same year.

One of the greatest writers dealing with the early Indians of Peru, and at the same time one of the least known, was Father Miguel Cabello de Balboa (b. ca. 1535) whose extensive manuscript entitled *Miscelánea antártica* belongs to the New York Public Library. The work has never been completely translated into any language, but in 1840 at Paris Henri Ternaux-Compans (1807-1864) edited and published a brief part of the manuscript under the title *Histoire du Pérou.* This was translated into Spanish and published at Madrid in 1920 under the title *Historia del Perú bajo la dominación de las Incas.* The author went to America in 1566, stopping first in Nueva Granada where he began his study of the natives and their origin. His manuscript was begun in 1576 and was completed at Lima in 1586.

A history based in part upon the author's experiences and compiled after considerable careful research is by Diego Fernández (b. ca. 1510). It is entitled *Primera y segunda parte de la historia del Perú,* and was published in two volumes in one in 1571 at Sevilla. It relates chiefly to the civil wars in Peru from 1543 to 1556, and in consequence the Council of the Indies forbade its being sent to America before 1729 and after 1731. The first part of the work appeared in a new edition of two volumes at Madrid in 1913 and 1914.

7. *La Plata*

A work dealing with La Plata region appeared in 1555 in Spanish under the title *Viaje al Río de la Plata* which recorded a journey made by the author, Ulrich Schmidel (ca. 1510-ca. 1579), during the years 1534 to 1554, part of which time he served as a soldier under Pedro de Mendoza. The volume describes the conquest of the region and the activities of Cabeza de Vaca. The first German edition appeared at Frankfurt-am-Main in 1567 under varying titles, one of which was *Warhafftige und liebliche beschreibung etlicher furnemen indianischen landtschafften und insulen.* An English translation may be found in volume LXXXI (original series, 1889) of the Hakluyt Society publications.

A work of historical value because of the events recorded, but written as a poem of 28 cantos of inferior quality, is *La Argentina y conquista del Río de la Plata, con otros acaecimientos de los reynos del Perú, Tucumán y estado del Brazil.* The author was Martín del Barco Centenera (1535-1604) who served as a soldier in the region. This is the first part of a projected larger work, of which no more was written. It covers the period from 1535 to about 1600 and was first printed at Lisboa in 1602. Two good Spanish editions appeared at Buenos Aires in 1836 and in 1912.

8. *Chile*

An interesting and, if properly used, a valuable historical account of the Araucanian wars in Chile may be found in the epic poem *La araucana,* written by Alonso de Ercilla y Zúñiga (1533-1594), a noble who as a youth had been a page at the marriage of Philip II to Mary Tudor and who later served under García Hurtado de Mendoza in the conflicts with the Araucanian Indians. The first part of the work was published at Madrid in 1569 and the second part appeared at the same place in 1578. The third part was first published in conjunction with the two preceding parts in 1590, also at Madrid. The poem was continued in two more parts by Diego de Santisteban Osorio (Salamanca, 1597), but its historical importance diminished with its numerous extensions. The poem has never been completely translated into English, but a very small part was translated by William Hayley (1745-1820) and H. Boyd and published at New York in 1808.

Another epic poem of a similar nature covering the same subject but supplementing *La araucana* and emphasizing the military aspects, is the *Primera parte de arauca domado* by Pedro de Oña (b. ca. 1570) published at Lima in 1596. A more recent edition is that which appeared at Santiago, Chile, in 1917. The second part was never written.

CHAPTER TWO

SEVENTEENTH CENTURY WORKS

A. Introduction
B. General works
  1. History, geography, description, etc.
  2. Religious accounts
  3. Voyages and travels
C. Works on individual countries and regions
  1. Brazil
  2. Mexico
  3. Florida
  4. Central America
  5. West Indies
  6. Tierra Firme
  7. Peru
  8. La Plata
  9. Chile

A. Introduction

Works relating to America written in the seventeenth century assumed a different character from those of the previous century, and dealt more with biography, description, religious accounts, and travel than previously. The Spanish and Portuguese by 1600 had very nearly reached the limits of their colonial holdings, and the respective governments began to consolidate their territories politically, economically, socially, and religiously, while at the same time they made vigorous efforts to defend their rich possessions from the attacks of jealous foreign aggressors. For this was a century when the English, French, Dutch, and Swedes took considerable interest in the New World, and their rivalry with the Iberian states resulted in freebooting, buccaneering, and open warfare. Travelers from Europe began to go to America for pleasure or profit and some of them recorded their experiences in frequently biased accounts, so that many of the so-called histories were in reality travel and descriptive accounts.

B. General Works

1. *History, Geography, Description, etc.*

Among the noteworthy general histories of this century which dealt with the Hispanic American world was the *Historia general de los hechos de los castellanos en las islas y tierra firme del mar océano* by Antonio de Herrera y Tordesillas (ca. 1549-1625). This work appeared at Madrid in eight volumes in four between 1601 and 1615, and the story was carried to the year 1555. The work is founded upon considerable documentary research since the author had been commissioned by Philip II to write the treatise. Yet certain parts of the history are taken literally from Las Casas. An English edition by John Stevens (d. 1726) was printed at London in 1725 and 1726 in six volumes. The best Spanish edition was published in eight volumes at Madrid in 1725. A new Spanish edition of eight or ten volumes is at present being published (1934 ff.) by the Academy of History at Madrid under the joint editorship of Antonio Ballesteros Beretta (b. 1880) and Angel de Altolaguirre y Duvale.

Another valuable and comprehensive work frequently cited is by Juan de Solórzano Pereira (1575-1655) usually given the title *De indiarum jure,* which appeared in Latin in two volumes at Madrid, the first volume being published in 1629 and the second in 1639. The first Spanish edition was published at Madrid in 1648 under a 275-word title briefly cited as *Política indiana.* The work is generally descriptive of the Indies and still constitutes a useful digest of laws and decrees applicable to the Spanish colonies.

A book of great erudition and of considerable interest to many because it brings together all of the theories concerning the origin of the American natives, but which at the same time is of little actual value, is the *Origen de los indios del nuevo mundo* by the Dominican Gregorio García, which was first published at Valencia in 1607. The author spent about twelve years in America as a missionary and came to the conclusion that the natives came originally from Asia and parts of the Old World. His writings and ideas are based partially upon his own observations and partially upon a manuscript written by a companion of Francisco Pizarro, Juan de Velanzos, which has never been published. García's volume was reprinted at Madrid in 1729, being edited by Andrés González Barcia Carballido y Zúñiga.

A work of somewhat similar nature appeared at Lima in 1681 under the title *Tratado única y singular del origen de los indios occidentales del Perú, México, Santa Fe y Chile.* The author, Diego Andrés Rocha, attempted to show the origen of the American natives and their relation to the lost Ten Tribes of Israel. The work was reprinted at Madrid in two volumes in 1891.

A very excellent and comprehensive work written in Peru between 1642 and 1653, but not published until 1890-95 when it appeared in four volumes at Sevilla, bore the title *Historia del nuevo mundo.* Its author was Bernabé Cobo de Peralta (1582-1657) who at the age of fourteen went to America to seek his fortune. In Peru he became a Jesuit and subsequently traveled widely collecting from observation many facts which he used in this history.

In 1625 appeared at Leyden a general descriptive treatise under the title *Nieuwe wereldt ofte beschrijvinghe van West-Indien* by Johannes de Laet (1593-1649), or Jean de Laet d'Anvers, as he is frequently called. The volume dealt with the natural history of America, with native customs, and with the establishment of colonies in the Western Hemisphere, all of which were treated in a careful manner. The book was republished in Latin at Leyden in 1633 under the title briefly cited as *Novus orbis.* It seems probable that the whole work was based upon the manuscript *Historia da America,* now lost, written by the Jesuit Manoel de Moraes (1586-1651).

A book biographical in nature is that by Francisco Pizarro y Orellana (d. ca. 1652) entitled *Varones ilustres de nuevo mundo* which appeared at Madrid in 1639. The author, who claimed to be a great-grandson of Francisco Pizarro, undertook this literary venture in order to defend the activities of the Pizarros in Peru and to solicit financial assistance for their descendants. Besides dealing with the conquerors of Peru, his book also tells the story of Cortés, Columbus, and others.

A work indispensable to economic and political historians, for it contains an abstract of the laws of the Indies, was published in two volumes at Sevilla in 1672 under the title *Norte de la contratación de las indias occidentales.* The author was José de Veitia Linaje (d. 1688). An indifferent English translation was made by John Stevens and published at London in one volume about 1700 under the title *The rule established in Spain for trade in the West Indies. . . .*

Another work of general nature, but of considerable importance, is the *Memorial noticias sacres y reales del imperio de las indias occidentales* by Juan Díez de la Calle published at Madrid in 1646. Somewhat similar in nature, but of greater length, is a volume by Alonso de la Peña Montenegro (d. 1688) entitled *Itinerario para parochos de indios* (Ambreses, 1698).

A general work with a misleading title is the *Reducción universal de todo el Perú* by the Dominican missionary, Miguel de Monsalve. This volume was written for the information of the Spanish king and was printed privately at Lima in 1604. Today only one copy is known. The author lived for thirty-seven years in Mexico, the West Indies, and South America, and no corruption or governmental defects seem to have escaped his attention.

A volume specialized in character is that by Antonio Rodríguez de León Pinelo (d. 1660) entitled *Tratado de confirmaciones reales de encomiendas oficios i casos* published at Madrid in 1630.

A work containing considerable tabulated information was published at Valencia in 1689 under the title of *Tablas cronológicas.* The author, who wrote under the pseudonym of Juan Eusebio Nieremberg, was Claude Clement (1594-1642), or as he is frequently called, Claudo Clemente. This work was based upon three separate publications (Zaragoza, 1676), one dealing with the Portuguese and two dealing with the Spanish discoveries and conquests to the year 1642.

A volume studied by all Spanish royal officials who went to America in the latter part of this century and in the one following was edited by Gaspar de Escalona y Agüero (d. 1659) under the title *Gazophilatium regium Perubicum.* It was published at Madrid in 1647 and was a compendium, written partly in Latin and partly in Spanish, of useful information about America. A second edition appeared in 1755.

German and Dutch accounts of the colonies are comparatively numerous. In 1612 at Cologne appeared a German work describing the discovery and exploration of America which bore the title *Indiæ occidentalis historia.* In 1618 the book was reprinted at the same place. The author was Gaspar Ens (b. ca. 1570). The work contains an account of the four voyages of Columbus, the expeditions of Cortés, Pizarro and others, and descriptions of Mexico, Central America, the West Indies, South America, and English and French North America. Another German work, by Johan Ludwig Gottfried, a collaborator with De Bry, was published at Frankfurt in 1655. Its title, running into nearly two hundred words, may be briefly cited as *Newe welt und americanische historien.*

A Dutch account, written by a person who used the pseudonym Athanasius Inga, appeared at Amsterdam in 1624 under the brief title *West-indische spieghel.* Another Dutch work entitled *Spieghel der australische navegatie* is by Jacob Le Maire (1585-1616) and was published at Amsterdam in 1622. A third Dutch account is by Arnoldus Montanus (ca. 1625-1683), who published at Amsterdam in 1671 his *De nieuwe en onbekende weereld* which treats mainly of the early discoveries made in America with special emphasis upon North America, the West Indies, and Brazil. An English volume based in part upon this book appeared at London the same year, its compiler being John Ogilby (1600-1676) and its title stated briefly is *America: being the latest and most accurate description of the new world.* This latter work was illustrated by fifty-seven plates and maps of considerable interest and value.

A brief French work of considerable interest was written by Samuel de Champlain (1567-1635) and published first in English under the title *Narrative of a voyage to the West Indies and Mexico in the years 1599-1602.* The translation was made from the original manuscript by Alice Wilmere and was published at London in 1858 by the Hakluyt Society as Volume XXIII of its First Series. Although the account is only 48 pages in length it contains valuable descriptions of the regions and some discussion of Spanish policy in America. The original manuscript drawings are reproduced in facsimile.

In 1614 at Madrid was published Pedro Ordóñez de Ceballos' (b. 1550) *Historia y viage del mundo,* a part of which relating to America was translated into Dutch and published at Amsterdam in 1621 under the title *Eyghentlijcke beschryvinghe van West-Indien.*

Among the chief and most familiar English descriptive works of the seventeenth century which concern Hispanic America is that by the English Dominican and later Protestant, Thomas Gage (d. 1656), usually entitled *A new survey of the West Indies.* However, when the book was first published at London in 1648 it appeared under the title *The English-American, his travail by sea and land.* Subsequent editions of this work have appeared at intervals, one of the most recent being at New York in 1929. The book deals not only with the West Indies but with Spanish North and South America, the author having spent twenty-four years in the Indies, especially in Mexico and Central America.

2. *Religious Accounts*

Some of the religious aspects of the conquest of America may be found in a work by Gaspar Plautius, an Austrian abbot, written anonymously under the title *Nova typis transacta navigatio* published in 1621, the place unknown.

A volume treating particularly the activities of the church in America and the conversion of the natives is entitled *Historia eclesiástica de nuestros tiempos.* The author was Alonzo Fernández and the book was printed at Toledo in 1611.

A work containing much interesting and valuable information concerning the early religious establishments in the Spanish colonies and the native Indian creeds is that by Gil González Dávila (1577-1658) entitled briefly *Teatro eclesiástico.* The first volume was published at Madrid in 1649 and the second at the same place in 1655.

Another religious account dealing especially with the West Indies and the north coast of South America is the *Relation des missiones de pp. de la compagnie de Jesus dans les isles, et dans la terra ferme de l'Amérique meridionale* (Paris, 1655) by Pierre Pelleprat (ca. 1606-1667). This also includes his *Introduction à la langue des Galibis. . .* published separately the same year at Paris.

3. *Voyages and Travels*

A type of English publication, of value to historians, which became especially popular in the next century was the compilation of accounts of voyages to various parts of the world. One of the briefest of these dealing with America appeared at London in 1699. It was edited by William Hacke and bore the title *A collection of original voyages,* some of which concerned Hispanic America.

An earlier and even more important collection of voyages made by Englishmen and others to America and elsewhere appeared in five volumes at London in 1625 and 1626 under the title *Hakluytus posthumous, or Purchas his pilgrimes.* The editor was Samuel Purchas (ca. 1577-1626). The fourth volume and parts of the third and fifth relate to voyages to America. Volume V had first appeared in 1613 under the title *Purchas his pilgrimage,* and it constituted in part an interesting account of the religions of the peoples of all countries. The whole work is an important yet miscellaneous assembly of accounts, some of which are of indifferent value. The most recent edition of this work in English appeared at Glasgow in twenty volumes from 1905 to 1907.

A French collection of voyages was made by Melchisedech Thévenot (ca. 1620-1696) under the title *Relations de divers voyages curieux* and was published in two volumes at Paris between 1663 and 1696. Four accounts contained in part four of the work relate to Spanish America, one of which had never before been published.

Among the volumes written in this century which deal with pirates, freebooters, and gentlemen adventurers in Hispanic America is the near-classic history by Alexandre Olivier Esquemelin (1645-1707), or John Esquemelin as he is often called (whose real name may have been Henrick Smeeks), which was first published at Amsterdam in 1674, or more probably in 1678, under the title *De americænsche zee-roovers.* This book has appeared in perhaps as many editions as has any book which deals with America. The first English edition was printed at London in two volumes in 1684 and 1685. One of the best English editions was published at London in 1893. The first Spanish edition appeared in 1681 at Colonia Agrippina and was followed by a second edition at the same place the next year.

A work of somewhat similar character, but dealing largely with piratical activities in the Pacific, appeared at Paris in 1689. It was by Raveneau de Lussan (b. 1663) and bore the title *Journal du voyage fait à la mer de sud.* The best and most recent English edition was published at Cleveland in 1930, and was translated and edited by Marguerite Eyer Wilbur.

C. Works on Individual Countries and Regions

1. *Brazil*

Several volumes dealing with Brazil should be cited. The first appeared at Valladolid in 1603 under the title *Historia general de la india oriental.* It was the work of the Benedictine monk, Antonio de San Román de Ribadeneyra, and dealt with the discovery and conquest of Brazil and other parts of the world in the sixteenth century. It constitutes one of the best records of the Portuguese explorers and their relations to contemporary events.

A second work was published in two volumes in one in 1628 at Madrid under the title *Epítome de las historias portuguesas.* The author was the poet and historian, Manuel de Faria e Sousa (1590-1648). His volumes treat Portuguese colonization to 1628 in Brazil as well as in the East, and are considered an excellent reference.

A third work appeared in 1627, the place of publication unknown, under the title *Historia da custodia do Brasil,* the author being the churchman Vicente do Salvador (ca. 1564-ca. 1639), the first historian of Brazil to be born there. In 1918 a new edition was published at São Paulo under the title *Historia do Brasil,* while a third edition appeared at the same place in 1931.

A fourth work, which contains much valuable information, was written in 1634 by Pedro Cudena but first appeared in 1780 at Braunschweig in German under the title *Beschreibung des portugiesischen Amerika.* The translator and editor was Christian Leiste.

A fifth work of importance, written by a Jesuit to show that the gold of Peru could be brought to the Atlantic by way of Brazil, is entitled *Nuevo descubrimiento del gran Río de Amazonas.* The author was Father Christóbal de Acuña (1597-1675), and the book appeared first at Madrid in 1641 but was soon suppressed by Philip IV for fear the Portuguese would use the idea. What seems to be a partial plagiarism appeared in French in 1656 at Paris under the title *Relation historique et geographique de la grande reviere des Amazones.* The work contains excerpts from various authors and was compiled by Blaise François, Comte de Pagan (d. 1665), who is usually cited as the author. The volume was translated and published in English in 1661 at London under the title *An historical and geographical description of the great country and river of the Amazones in America.* The first English translation of the whole work appeared at London in 1698 under the title *Voyages and discoveries in South America.* The Hakluyt Society published a translation as part of Volume XXIV, first series (London, 1859).

A sixth work, concerning the Dutch in Brazil, appeared at Paris in 1651 under the title *Histoire des derniers troubles du Brésil entre les Hollendois et les Portugais.* The author was Pierre Moreau.

A seventh work of narrow scope covering the decade 1634-1644 and written from material furnished by the Dutch governor, Maurice of Nassau, was by Gaspar Barlaeius (1584-1648), or Kaspar van Boerle as he is often called, and it bore the title *Rerum per octennium in Brasilia, et alibi gestarum . . . historia.* This book was published at Clivis in 1660 and formed the basis of all subsequent histories of this period. The first edition of the work appeared in 1647, the place not known. A recent Dutch edition was published at Gravenhage in 1923.

An eighth work is entitled *Noticias curiosas e necessarias das cousas do Brasil,* and was written by the Jesuit Simão de Vasconcellos (ca. 1611-1671). It appeared at Lisbon in 1668 but it contained much of the material found in his earlier and more important work entitled *Chronicas da Companhia de Jesus na provincia do Brasil* (Lisbon, 1663).

A ninth volume treating of the discovery and early history of Brazil is Francisco de Brito Freyre's (1620-1692) *Nova Lusitania,* published at Lisbon in 1675. Part of the book, which dealt with the Dutch in Brazil, was written from observations made while the author served as admiral of the Portuguese fleet.

A tenth work, by the Benedictine Raphael de Jesús (1614-1693) entitled *Castrioto lusitano,* was published at Lisbon in 1679 and dealt thoroughly with the Dutch in Brazil between 1623 and 1654. Only the first part of the work has ever been published.

An eleventh volume which summarizes the occupation and spiritual domination of a large part of Brazil bears the title *El Marañón y Amazonas* (Madrid, 1684). The author was Manuel Rodríguez (1633-1701), the Jesuit Procurator General of the Indies at Madrid, who wrote his account from the documents found in the government archives of that city.

A twelfth work of extreme value for the student of early seventeenth century conditions in Brazil is the anonymous *Dialogos das grandezas do Brasil,* written in the form of conversations between two persons living in the country. An incomplete edition was published serially in *Isis* (January 1848 to June 1849) at Rio de Janeiro. João Capistrano de Abreu (1853-1927) published a new and better edition in the *Diario Official* at Rio de Janeiro (February to March 1900). The best edition appeared at Rio de Janeiro in 1930, being edited by Rodolpho Garcia.

2. *Mexico*

Mexico, or New Spain, was the subject of many historical and descriptive treatises in the seventeenth century, only a few of the most important of which can be cited. Either in 1613 at Madrid or in 1615 at Sevilla the three-volume *Monarquía indiana* by the Franciscan Juan de Torquemada (1550-1625) was published dealing with the natives and antiquities of New Spain. The best edition of this work with changes and corrections appeared at Madrid in three volumes in 1723.

An account of the conquest of New Spain written in this century is by the literary but rather inaccurate historian, Antonio de Solís y Rivadeneyra (1610-1686), whose *Historia de la conquista de México* was first published at Madrid in 1684 in one volume which carries the story to the capture of Guatimozin. The work was continued in a second volume to the death of Cortés by Ignacio de Salazar y Olarte (d. 1786) under the same title (Córdoba, 1743). One of the best two-volume editions was published at Madrid in 1785. An English translation of the first volume was published at London in 1724.

In 1637 appeared at Mexico City the *Relación universal legítima* by Fernando de Cepeda which, after the corrections and additions made by Juan de Alvarez Serrano, dealt with the founding of Mexico City and described that country during the years 1553 to 1637.

A work following somewhat the same theme bears the title *Obediencia que México, cabeza de la Nueva España, dió á la majestad católica del rey D. Felipe de Austria.* It was written by Arias de Villalobos (b. ca. 1568) and was published at Mexico City in 1623. An edition edited by Genaro García appeared in 1907.

A general descriptive account of New Spain can be found in Agustín de Vetancurt's (1620-1700) *Teatro mexicano* published in 1697 or 1698 in two volumes at Mexico City. A four-volume edition of this work appeared at Mexico City in 1870 and 1871. Another general descriptive work of considerable value on life in New Spain appeared as Volume VI of the *Giro del mondo* (6 vols., Naples, 1699-1721) by Giovanni Francesco Gemelli Careri, (1651-1725). This volume was translated into Spanish as *Viaje a la Nueva España* by José María de Agreda y Sánchez (1838-1916) and was published at Mexico City in 1927. Still another descriptive work, probably written early in the century, is *Descripción geográphica de los reynos de Galicia, Vizcaya, y Nueva León* by Alonso de la Mota y Escobar (1546-1625). It was finally published from a manuscript copy at Mexico City in 1930. A second edition appeared at the same place in 1940.

A valuable account of the activities of the Jesuits in New Spain, particularly in Sinaloa, California, and Florida, and with their conversion of the natives, is by the Jesuit Andrés Pérez de Ribas (d. 1655) who wrote the *Historia de los triunfos de nuestra santa fé entre gentes las más bárbaras y fieras del nuevo orbe.* It was published at Madrid in 1645. Another account of Jesuit activities in the region is given by the prolific writer, Francisco de Florencia (1619-1695), under the title *Historia de la provincia de la Compañía de Jesús de Nueva España* published at Mexico City in 1649.

An account of the Augustinians in New Spain and particularly in Michoacán is found in the *Historia de la provincia de San Nicolás de Tolentino de Michoacán* by Diego Basalenque (b. 1577), the chronicler of the Order, who died in 1651. His work, however, did not appear until 1673, the place of publication being unknown. Another account of Augustinian activities, especially between 1523 and 1592, is entitled *Crónica de la orden de N.P.S. Augustín en los provincias de la Nueva España* (Mexico, 1624), by Juan de Grijalva (ca. 1559-1638).

A Franciscan work, written about 1653, is generally cited as the *Chronica miscelanea* and was by Antonio Tello (b. ca. 1596). This was arranged in three parts, the first dealing with the Indians of New Spain, the second dealing with the conquest of New Spain, and the third giving the biographies of Franciscan missionaries. The first part was not published until 1890 at Guadalajara, Mexico, while the second part appeared the next year at the same place. In the latter volume chapters CCLXXVII to CCC seem to have been composed by Fray Jaime de Rieza Gutiérrez. Part three was never published.

The activities of the Order of Predicadores is told by Francisco de Burgoa (1605-1681) in his *Palestra historial de virtudes y exemplares apostólicos* (Mexico, 1670). The latest edition of this work was printed at Mexico

City in 1934. A second work by the same author appeared at Mexico City in 1674 under the title briefly cited as *Geográfica descripción. . . .* It deals with Oaxaca chiefly. A new edition was published at Mexico City in two volumes in 1934.

Religious activities in Guadalajara are described by Alonso Núñez de Castro (b. 1627) under the title *Historia eclesiástica y seglar de la muy noble y muy leal ciudad de Gudalaxara* (Madrid, 1653).

A number of works which deal in part with the conquest of the Indians were written in this century, some of which, however, did not appear in print until later. Among these is a curious work in praise of the American natives and in particular of the natives of New Spain somewhat in the manner of Las Casas. It is by Bishop Juan de Palafox y Mendoza (1600-1659) entitled briefly *Virtudes del indio* and was published perhaps at Madrid probably in 1650. The book was addressed to the king in order to show him the nature and extent of the Spanish mistreatment of the Indians. It was printed secretly. A second small edition was published at Zaragoza in 1661 under the title *Historia de las virtudes del indio.* A recent edition appeared in Madrid in 1893.

In 1828 at Mexico City appeared the seventeenth century work entitled the *Horribles crueldades de los conquistadores de México,* by Fernando de Alva Ixtlilzochitl (ca. 1568-1648).

A work in French entitled *Histoire du Mexique,* written in this century by Fernando Alvarado Tezózomoc, appeared at Paris in two volumes between 1847 and 1849. It deals mainly with the origin of the natives of New Spain. A Spanish edition appeared at Mexico City in 1878.

In 1914 at Madrid was published Diego Luis de Motezumas' (1619-1699) seventeenth century *Corona mexicana, ó historia de los nueve Montezumas.*

A story in verse of the conquest of New Mexico, together with an excellent description of the native inhabitants, may be found in the *Historia de la Nueva México* by Gaspar Pérez de Villagrá (1555-1620), published at Alcalá in 1610 and at Mexico City in two volumes in 1910. An English translation of this account was made by Gilberto Espinosa and printed by the Quivira Society at Los Angeles in 1933. A religious history of the same region is the *Crónica* by the Franciscan Balthasar de Medina (1635-1697), published at Mexico City in 1682 giving numerous biographies of Franciscan martyrs in Mexico. A description of New Mexico about 1600, together with a brief account of the *entradas* of the region, was written by Juan de Montoya, a learned priest, under the title *Relación del descubrimiento del Nueva México* (Rome, 1602). An English translation was made by George Peter Hammond and Agapito Rey under the title *New Mexico in 1602 . . .* (Albuquerque, 1938).

Of seventeenth century histories dealing with Yucatan, mention may be made of those by Bernardo de Lizana (d. 1631) entitled *Historia de Yucatán* (Mexico, 1633), and by Diego López de Cogolludo (1610-1686) entitled *Historia de Yucatán* (Madrid, 1688). In 1867-68 a third edition of this treatise was published at Mérida in two volumes. Of the two works the latter is much the better since the author had the use of considerable documentary material. Another volume on Yucatan of this period is entitled *Relación historial eclesiástica de la provincia de Yucatán de la Nueva España, escrita el año de 1639* by Francisco de Cárdenas Valencia. The book was printed at Mexico City in 1937.

3. *Florida*

The chief work on Florida in this century was written by the Peruvian Franciscan Luis Gerónimo de Oré (1554-1629) under the title *Relación de los Mártires que ha habido en la Florida.* It was published in Spain, the exact place being unknown, some time between 1617 and 1620. The book is of value in showing the work of the early missionaries between 1595 and 1616. A recent Spanish edition appeared at Madrid in 1931, while an English translation was made by Rev. Maynard Geiger and published at New York in 1936.

4. *Central America*

One of the chief works dealing with Central America in this century is the *Historia de la provincia de S. Vicente de Chyapa y Guatemala* which deals with religious and other matters. It was written by Fray Antonio de Remesal (1570-1639) and appeared at Madrid in 1619. A new edition of this work with the 1619 title page appeared at Guatemala in two volumes in 1932. In 1620 at Madrid appeared an edition of the 1619 work with a title page reading *Historia general de las indias occidentales. . . .* Another important work written in this period but not published until later was the *Historia de Guatemala* by Francisco Antonio de Fuentes y Guzmán (1643-ca. 1699), two volumes, Madrid, 1882 and 1883.

5. *West Indies*

A work dealing largely with the natives of the West Indies and particularly with the Caribs is that by Guillaume Coppier (ca. 1600-1670) entitled briefly *Histoire et voyage des indes occidentales* published at Lyons in 1645. An English volume dealing with the West Indies and with many other parts of America, as well, appeared at London in 1655 under the initials N. N. and the title *America: or an exact description of the West Indies.* The aim of the author seems to have been to advertise to English readers the history and importance of the Spanish islands.

A French description of the West Indies is entitled *Histoire naturelle et morale des Isles Antilles de l'Amerique. . . .*(Rotterdam?, 1658) by Charles de Rochefort (b. 1605) and not by Cesar de Rochefort, as is often asserted. Editions have appeared in Dutch and German, but not in Spanish or in English.

6. *Tierra Firme*

Tierra Firme was treated in this century by Lucas Fernández de Piedrahita (1624-1688) in his careful and eloquent *Historia general de las conquistas del nuevo reyno de Granada,* the first part of which appeared at Antwerp in 1688 and carried the account to the year 1563. The volume is written largely from the manuscripts left by Gonzalo Jiménez de Quesada (ca. 1500-1579) which have never been completely published.

An earlier book which dealth with the same territory is entitled *Primera parte de las noticias historiales de las conquistas de tierra firme en las indias occidentales* by Pedro Simón (b. 1574). It was published at Cuenca in 1627. Parts two and three of this work were not printed entirely until they appeared at Bogotá in 1882. In 1891 and 1892 parts one, two, and three were published at Bogotá in four volumes. Part four was lost and never printed.

An interesting and often quoted work treating the Panama isthmus in this century is by the English surgeon Lionel Wafer (ca. 1660-ca. 1705) entitled *A new voyage and description of the isthmus of America, giving an account of the officer's abode there. . .* , first published at London in 1699. A second edition with additions appeared at London in 1704, while a third edition was published in Volume III of Dampier's, *A collection of voyages* (London, 1729). The book was early translated and printed in other languages, the first French edition appearing at Paris in 1706. The best English edition is to be found in the Hakluyt Society publications, Second Series, Volume LXXIII (Oxford, 1934), while the best United States edition is that edited by George Parker Winship and published at Cleveland in 1903.

7. *Peru*

The most important work in any language dealing with the conversion of the Indians of Peru is that by the Jesuit Pablo José de Arriaga (ça. 1562-1622), entitled *Extirpación de la idolatría del Perú,* published at Lima in 1621. This earliest edition of the book, of which there are only two copies known, contains 156 pages and the Cortes Society, before it expired, planned to publish an English translation. The author went to Peru about 1583 and became one of the leading educators in the colony.

A valuable work dealing with the activities of the Augustinian Order in Peru is by Antonio de la Calancha (1584-1654) entitled *Crónica moralizada del orden de San Augustín en el Perú, con sucesos ejemplares* (Barcelona, 1638). The work, however, is not exclusively confined to Peru proper but includes present-day Chile, Ecuador, and Colombia, and deals also in a somewhat confused manner with economic and political affairs of historical importance from 1551 to 1593. The work was continued later to 1657 by Bernardo de Torres (d. ca. 1660) in his *Crónica de la provincia peruana del orden de los ermitaños de S. Augustín* (Lima, 1657).

A Jesuit historian about whom there is much controversy concerning the accuracy of his work is the credulous and naïve Fernando Montesinos (b. ca. 1600), who went to Peru about 1629 and remained until at least 1642. Generally he seems to have repeated many facts as they came to him with little or no investigation. However, he preserved much valuable information in his *Memorias antiguas historiales y políticas del Perú* (Buenos Aires, 1870) which deals with the pre-conquest period, and in his *Los anales del Perú* (2 vols., Madrid, 1906) which covers the post-conquest period. The first work appeared in French at Paris in 1840 as Volume XVII of Henri Ternaux-Compans' *Voyages* . . . , and was published in English translation by the Hakluyt Society in 1920 as Volume XLVIII (second series). A Spanish edition edited by Marcos Jiménez de la Espada was published at Madrid in 1882. The complete work as planned by the author under the title *Ophir de España* has never been printed in any language.

Still another work dealing with religious affairs in Peru in particular and with political conditions etc. elsewhere in South America was published at Rome in three volumes in 1681 and 1682 under the title *Tesoros verdaderos de las indias en la historia de la gran provincia de San Juan Bautista del Perú, de el orden de predicadores.* The author was Juan de Meléndez, a native-born Peruvian.

8. *La Plata*

Paraguay as a center of Jesuit activity was treated by Nicolás del Techo (1611-1680) in a book entitled *Historia provinciæ Paraguariæ societatis Jesu,* first published in Latin at Leodii (i. e., Liége) in 1673. An abridged English translation appeared in 1704 in Volume IV of Awnsham Churchill's (d. 1728) *A collection of voyages and travels.* Another volume dealing with the same region and the same subject was by the Jesuit Antonio Ruiz de Montoya (ca. 1593-ca. 1652) entitled *Conquista espiritual hecha por los religiosos de la Compañia de Jesús en las provincias del Paraguay* (Madrid, 1639). The author, who converted over 100,000 Indians, bitterly criticizes the Spaniards for their treatment of the natives. His book is written from memory and in an ill-arranged fashion, but is nevertheless of great value.

Another volume dealing with the Paraguay district is entitled *Insignes misioneros de la Compañia de Jesús en la provincia del Paraguay.* The author was Francisco Xarque (1609-91), honorary chaplain of the Spanish king, rector of Potosí, and a Peruvian judge. His book was published at Pamplona in 1687.

Still another work dealing with the Jesuits in the region, and especially with the native customs, was written by two German Jesuits, Antonio Sepp and Antonio Bohm. This entertaining account is entitled *Reiszbeschreibung wie dieselbe aus Hispanien in Paraquarian kommen*. It was printed at Nuremberg first probably in 1696.

9. *Chile*

The chief historical and descriptive work relating to Chile written in this century bears the title *Histórica relación del reyno de Chile* and the author is Alonso de Ovalle (d. 1650). It was published at Rome in 1646 at the same time that an abridged Italian edition appeared there. The Spanish edition contains twenty-one engraved portraits of important Spaniards connected with early Chilean history, and treats of the activities of the Jesuits in the region. Part of the work (the first six books out of eight) was translated into English and printed at London in 1703 in Churchill's *A collection of voyages and travels*.

CHAPTER THREE

EIGHTEENTH CENTURY WORKS

A. Introduction

B. General works

1. History, geography, discription, etc.
2. Religious accounts
3. Voyages and travels

C. Works on individual countries and regions

1. Brazil
2. Mexico
3. Texas
4. Florida
5. California
6. Central America
7. West Indies
8. Tierra Firme
9. Peru
10. La Plata
11. Chile

A. Introduction

The eighteenth century saw the publication of an ever increasing number of works relating to Hispanic America, a large portion of which were description and travel accounts (here generally omitted for lack of space), many of them of the sixteenth and seventeenth centuries and printed for the first time. These were almost invariably edited and compiled in collections numbering several volumes. General histories were numerous but they were frequently contentious and partisan; particularly is this true of religious accounts and of works treating nationalism. The French and English became sufficiently interested in Hispanic America to write histories in increasing numbers, while the Germans, Dutch, and Italians lost some of their interest in America.

During the century numerous European controversies which were both the cause and result of economic, social, and political theorizing, affected the literary output of both Europeans and Americans. Besides, the approach of revolutionary changes likewise affected published views and opinions and pseudo-histories. In consequence a judicial use of certain eighteenth century works is obviously necessary.

B. General Works

1. *History, Geography, Description, etc.*

Among the general works relating to Hispanic America the following should be mentioned. Between 1768 and 1770 Antoine Touron (1686-1775) published his fourteen-volume *Histoire générale de l'Amérique depuis sa découverte.* A few years later a five-volume comprehensive work entitled *Diccionario geográfico-histórico de las indias occidentales ó América* by Antonio de Alcedo y Bexarano (1736-1812) was printed at Madrid between 1786 and 1789. The work was translated into English and published, with additions by G. A. Thomson, at London in five volumes in 1812-15.

A careful work, written from the documents but never finished, is that by Juan Bautista Múñoz (1745-1799) entitled *Historia del nuevomundo* which appeared at Madrid in 1793. Four years later (1797) an English edition was published at London. During 1940 this work was reprinted in the *Boletín* del Archivo General de la Nación at Ciudad Trujillo.

Another valuable volume which is in reality a preliminary sketch of a larger one never written is that by Lorenzo Boturini Benaducci (ca. 1702-1750) entitled *Idea de una nueva historia general de la América septentrional,* published at Madrid in 1746. The book deals largely with the natives of Mexico, and is based upon many manuscripts contained in monasteries of that country, where the author resided for eight years.

A work of less importance is that briefly entitled *Investigaciones históricas* by Cristóbal Cladera (1760-1816) published at Madrid in 1794, which describes the principal sea discoveries made by the Spanish in the fifteenth and the early sixteenth centuries.

Another author of this century often referred to is Antonio de Ulloa (1716-1795) whose *Noticias americanas* published at Madrid in 1772 is considered a storehouse of facts regarding Spanish America, and particularly Peru and Ecuador. An important volume of a different nature appeared at Madrid in 1748 by Jorge Juan y Santacilia (1703-1773) entitled *Observaciones astronómicas y fisicas.* This work usually appears in conjunction with Ulloa's four-volume (Madrid, 1748) *Relación histórica del viage á la América meridional hecho de orden de S. Magestad.* An English translation in two volumes is dated 1758 and was published at London under the title of *A voyage to South America.* A special treatise jointly prepared by the authors for the king under the title *Noticias secretas de América* which gives a most thorough picture of colonial affairs was kept in the royal archives until it appeared in modified form in print at London, two volumes in one, in 1826. Later editions of this work have frequently appeared under the title *Popery judged by its fruits.*

A number of general works relating to Hispanic America were written by Englishmen in this century. Of these *The history of America* by William

Robertson (1721-1793) published at London in two volumes in 1777 stands at the forefront. Two other volumes of less merit are by William Russell (1741-1793) entitled *The history of America* (2 vols., London, 1777-78) and an earlier volume by Richard Rolt (ca. 1725-1770) which bore the title *A new and accurate history of South America* (London, 1756). A projected second volume by the last author dealing with North America did not appear. A fourth work, attributed to Edmund Burke (ca. 1729-1797), was published in London in two volumes in 1757 under the title *An account of the European settlements in America.* Only a part of the account (part three and chapters VII-XI) deals with Spanish America.

A volume earlier than these, appearing in London in 1741, bore the title *A concise history of the Spanish America.* The author is supposed to have been Dr. John Campbell (1708-1775). The book is comprehensive in treatment but with special emphasis upon trade and commercial conditions. The same writer is also supposed to be the author of the anonymous work entitled *The Spanish Empire in America* published at London in 1747, dealing with discovery, settlement, etc. In reality this work seems to be a second edition of the volume published in 1741.

Two anonymous works whose authorship has not been definitely fixed are *An account of the Spanish settlements in America,* published at London and Edinburgh in 1762, and *A description of the Spanish islands and settlements on the coast of the West Indies,* published at London in the same year. The latter work is usually attributed to Thomas Jefferys (d. 1771) who aimed to call England's attention to rich Spanish possessions at a time when the two countries were at war with each other.

A different but interesting and valuable book for historians is entitled *The American atlas: or a geographical description of the whole continent of America,* published at London in 1778. It was the work of a number of collaborators.

Works dealing with more special aspects of Hispanic American history are numerous in the eighteenth century. In 1749 at Cádiz appeared a volume entitled *Tratado histórico* by José Gutiérrez de Rubalcava which concerned all aspects of Spain's commerce with the Indies. At Amsterdam in 1770 appeared the four volumes of the Abbé Guillaume Thomas François Raynal (1713-1796) entitled *Analyse de l'histoire philosophique et politique des établissements et des commerces des Européens dans les deux indes.* An English edition in four volumes was published at London in 1776 while a Spanish edition in five volumes appeared at Madrid between 1784 and 1790. Another work treating matters of a commercial nature appeared at Madrid in 1797. It was entitled briefly *Memorias históricas* and was written by Rafael Antúñez y Acevedo, a pseudonym for João Antonio Andreoni (1650-1716). Still another work, more theoretical in nature, was by Gerónimo de Uztáriz (d. ca. 1750) published at Madrid in 1724 under the title *Teórica y práctica de comercio.* A work both critical and suggestive of the economic and social conditions in the Indies was published at Madrid in 1789, although it had been written in 1748, under the title briefly cited *Nuevo sistema de gobierno económico para la América.* The author was José del Campillo y Cosío (1693-1743).

An interesting work of a different nature in three volumes is that by Andrés Gonzáles Barcia Carballido y Zúñiga entitled briefly *Historiadores primitivos.* It was published at Madrid in 1749 and consists of a collection of relations, histories, etc., of the Spanish conquest in America.

A great many books in this century dealt with the treatment of the natives, and with their history, origin, etc. Many of these were naturally controversial or theoretical in nature. Such a work originally written in Italian by Giovanni (or Juan) Nuix (1740-1783) under the title *Reflessioni imparziali* was translated into Spanish by Pedro Varela y Ulloa (1748-1795) under the title *Reflexiones imparciales sobre la humanidad de los españoles en las indias* (Madrid, 1782). This work aimed mainly to defend the Spaniards from the calumnies of their enemies.

A work of special interest and emphasis, which appeared in this century, was entitled *Les Incas, ou la destruction de l'empire du Pérou* by Jean François Marmontel (1723-1799). The book was published at Berne in 1777 in two volumes in French. The same year a two-volume English edition was printed at London. In 1794 a three-volume French edition appeared at Paris. Many subsequent editions have been issued in several languages.

2. *Religious Accounts*

In this century many volumes were written concerning religious matters, and particularly about the Jesuits who were expelled by the Portuguese in 1760 and by the Spanish in 1767.

The most extensive history dealing with ecclesiastical affairs appeared at Paris in fourteen volumes in 1768-70. It was the *Histoire générale de l'Amérique* by Antoine Touron, already referred to.

A volume indispensable to the student of the church and the *patronato real* in America is the *Manual compendio del regio patronato indiano* by Antonio Joaquín de Ribadeneira y Barrientos (b. 1710) which contains all of the papal bulls relating to this subject from the time of Alexander VI to the date of its publication at Madrid in 1755. A second work very similar in nature, with edicts and decrees of the Spanish kings and of the popes concerning ecclesiastical administration in the Spanish colonies, is the *Fasti novi orbis et ordinationum apostolicarium ad indias pertinetium brevarium cum adnotationibus* by the Jesuit Domingo Muriel (1718-1795) who wrote under the pseudonym of Cyriac Moral. The book was first published at

Venice in 1776 and is considered an excellent source for the secular as well as church legislation in the Indies.

Among the works dealing particularly with the Jesuits several should be mentioned. In 1741 at Madrid appeared the *Historia de la provincia de la Compañía de Jesús* by José Cassani (1673-1750) which treated the activities of the Order in northern South America. Some years later, in 1783, appeared the *Gobierno de los regulares de la América* by Pedro José Parras (d. 1787), the rector and chancellor of the University of Tucumán. It was published at Madrid in two volumes and deals largely with the Jesuits in southern South America. A German account of the Jesuits under the title *Reisen einiger missionariem der gesellschaft Jesu in Amerika* appeared at Nürnberg in 1785. The author was Christoph Gottlieb von Murr (1733-1811).

An Italian work dealing with the Jesuits in Paraguay is that by Ludovico Antonio Muratori (1672-1750). It contains a long title frequently cited as *Il Cristianesimo felice . . . nel Paraguai* (2 vols., Venice, 1743-49). This is based upon two earlier accounts by the same author never before published together. The work was translated into English under the title *A relation of the missions of Paraguay* (London, 1759). A French edition with the same title in French had been printed at Paris in 1754. The author and compiler was not a Jesuit, and the work has been considered by many as impartial for that reason.

Two works in Spanish dealing with the Jesuits in Paraguay may be mentioned. The first appeared at Madrid in two volumes in 1726 under the title *Relación historial. . . .* The author, who was Juan Patricio Fernández (1661-1733), gives considerable information concerning the activities of the Jesuits and of the character of the Chiquitos Indians. The work has been widely translated. A second, and far better though little known, work is entitled *Historia de la Compañía de Jesús en la provincia del Paraguay.* It was also published at Madrid in two volumes during 1754 and 1755. The author was the Jesuit Pedro Lozano (d. ca. 1752), one of "the most prolific and trustworthy" of the Jesuit writers on Paraguay. His work covers only twenty-eight years of the region's history ending in 1614, and it seems to have been based in part at least upon two volumes of a work now lost written by Father Pastor (d. 1658).

The best and most authentic account of the Franciscans in America which appeared in this century is the *Crónica de la seráfica religión* by José Torrubia (ca. 1700-ca. 1768). This volume contains the important "Book One" of the ninth part of the author's chronicle and deals with the activities of the Order chiefly in America. The work was published at Rome in 1756. The author served as a missionary in both the Philippines and New Spain, and wrote his history from observations and documents largely from the missionary point of view and, in consequence, with some prejudice.

3. *Voyages and Travels*

The eighteenth century saw the compiling of many histories and collections of travels and voyages. The following do not, however, constitute a complete list.

In 1704 at London Awnsham Churchill published the first four volumes of *A collection of voyages and travels* previously mentioned. In 1732 were added two more volumes. In 1744 the work was revised and brought down to date in six volumes, while the next year saw the addition of the Osborne or Oxford collection to the original Churchill edition to make it more complete. A competing series was issued at London in 1705 by John Harris (1667-1719) in two volumes under the title *Navigantium atque itinerantium bibliotheca.* It was reprinted at London from 1744 to 1748 with additions and revisions. It differed from Churchill's largely because it was a history of travels rather than a collection of travels.

In 1706 and 1707 at Leyden, Pieter van der Aa (d. 1730) issued his *Naaukeurige versameling der gedink-waardigste zee en land-reysen na oost en West-Indiën* in 127 volumes containing accounts of voyages to all parts of the world. These have all been issued separately. In the same year (1707) M. du Perier published at Paris his *Histoire universelle des voyages.* This collection appeared in English at London in 1708, but in 1710 it was given a new title and the author did not use his pseudonym but was called the Abbé Bellegarde whose full name was Jean Baptiste Morvan de Bellegarde (1648-1734). The volume related to Spanish voyages to America and consisted of accounts taken from Spanish authors.

At Paris between 1746 and 1789 appeared 20 volumes under the general title *Histoire générale des voyages* covering voyages by land and sea written in different languages. The compiler was the Abbé Antoine François Prévost d'Exiles (1697-1763). Volumes XII, XIII, XIV, and XV deal with America.

An extensive collection of voyages in 32 volumes (Paris, 1780-1801) is entitled *Abrégée de l'histoire générale des voyages.* This is in part an abridgement of Prévost's work. The first 23 volumes were compiled by Jean-François de La Harpe (1739-1803). Volumes 24 to 32 inclusive were added by Victor Delpuech de Comeiras (1733-1805).

A collection issued in 42 volumes (Paris, ca. 1767-95) bore the title *Le voyageur François* . . . and covered the Old and New Worlds. Volumes 1 to 26 were compiled by the Abbé Joseph de Leporte (1713-1779), sometimes written Deleporte. Volumes 27 and 28 were by L. A. de B. de Fontenoy (1737-1806), while volumes 29 to 42 were by Louis Domairon (1745-1807). Several editions of various volumes have been published subsequently.

A collection first published in 20 volumes (London, 1796-97) was called *Historical account of the most celebrated voyages and travels from the time of Columbus.* It was compiled by William Fordyce Mavor (1758-1837). A new and better edition was published at London in 1810 in 28 volumes with the title *General collection of voyages and travels.*

Another pretentious collection bore the title *The world displayed.* It was published at London in 20 volumes between 1759 and 1761 and it contained the accounts of the early discoveries of the Spanish, Portuguese, French, and English in America and other parts of the world.

A briefer collection of voyages was compiled by the English buccaneer, William Dampier (1652-1715), under the French title *Collection de voyages* which was published at Paris in five volumes in 1715, and in English at London under the title *A collection of voyages.* Each of the volumes contains material on Hispanic America. The best English edition was published at London in four volumes in 1729. These volumes are based upon Dampier's *A new voyage round the world* (London, 1697) and upon accounts written by others.

Three other collections may be noted. In December 1708 there began to appear monthly *A new collection of voyages and travels* compiled under the editorship of John Stevens. By 1710 the collection included two volumes. In 1770 and 1771 at London appeared in two volumes *An historical collection of the several voyages and discoveries in the south Pacific Ocean* by Alexander Dalrymple (1737-1808), the first volume of which contained accounts of a number of Spanish voyages. In 1756 Charles de Brosses (1709-1777) brought out in two volumes at Paris his *Histoire des navigations aux terres australes* which was translated into several languages, the first English edition appearing in 1766 under the title *Terra australis cognita.*

C. Works on Individual Countries and Regions

1. *Brazil*

Histories concerning Brazil are numerous but are frequently of no great importance in this century. The chief general treatise, however meagre and inaccurate, although based upon much documentary material, is the *Historia da America portugueza* by the Brazilian Sebastião da Rocha Pitta (1660-1738), published at Lisbon in 1730. This work, shortly suppressed by the Portuguese government, covered the period from 1500 to 1724. Another work, which has a misleading title, is the *Histoire des découvertes et conquêtes des Portugais dans le nouveau monde* by the Jesuit Joseph François Lafitau (ca. 1670-ca. 1740) published at Paris in two volumes in 1732. This work deals almost exclusively with the Portuguese in Asia and Africa, although it does concern early Portuguese voyages to America. The same work was republished at Paris in 1734 in four volumes.

A volume frequently considered of great value in Brazilian history but of narrow scope is the *Annaes historicos do estado do Maranhão* by Bernardo

Pereira de Berredo (d. 1748), published at Lisbon in 1749. The author was governor of Maranhão between 1718 and 1748 and his history covers the period from the discovery to 1718.

Another brief account is by José Joaquim da Cunha de Azevedo Coutinho (ca. 1743-1821) entitled variously *Ensaio economico sobre o commercio de Portugal e suas colonias* and *Analyse sobre a justiça do commercio.* It was published at Lisbon in 1794, and deals with the trade and economic conditions of Brazil. An English translation appeared at London in 1807 under the title *An essay on the commerce and products of the Portuguese colonies in South America, especially the Brazils.*

Another economic treatise of considerable excellence appeared at Lisbon in 1711. It was written by João Antonio Andreoni, who wrote under the pseudonyms of André Antonio Antonil and Rafael Antúñez y Acevedo, and bore the title *Cultura e opulencia do Brasil por suas drogas e minas.* So revealing was this volume of the colony's wealth that the Portuguese government suppressed it and all but a few copies were destroyed. The latest edition in Portuguese was published at São Paulo and Rio de Janeiro in 1923.

A work of general description, valuable especially for the Amazon basin, was written by Charles Marie de La Condemine (1701-1774), who was sent on a French scientific expedition to Peru and who returned by way of the Amazon River. His work bears the title *Relation abrégée d'un voyage fait dans l'interieur de l'Amérique méridionale* (Paris, 1745). An English edition appeared at London in 1747 entitled *A succinct abridgement of a voyage made within the inland parts of South-America.* A Spanish edition appeared at Madrid in 1935. The report of the whole scientific journey was printed at Paris in 1751 under the title *Journal du voyage fait par ordre du roi à l'equateur. . . .*

An extensive and valuable work dealing with the country in eleven volumes appeared at Lisbon between 1789 and 1806. It bore the title *O fazendeiro do Brasil* and was by José Mariano da Conceição Velloso Xavier (1742-1811).

A large but anonymous work is entitled *Historia dos descobrimentos e conquistas dos Portuguezes no novo mundo.* It was published in four volumes at Lisbon in 1786 and 1787 and covers the period from Manoel I to João IV.

The most valuable accounts of the Franciscans in Brazil are the *Primazia serafica na regiam da America* by Appollinario da Conceição (1692-ca. 1760) published at Lisbon in 1733, and the *Orbe serafico novo brasilico* by Antonio de Santa Maria Jaboatão (b. 1695), the chronicler of the Order, published at Lisbon in 1761. The second part of this work finally appeared in a complete edition with the first part at Rio de Janeiro between 1858 and 1862. It was in five volumes.

A valuable ecclesiastical history of Brazil from the viewpoint of the Jesuits is the *Brasilia pontificia* by the Jesuit Simón Marques (b. 1684), published at Lisbon in 1758. The author went to Brazil in 1702 and held a number of important positions, including that of rector of the Jesuit college at Rio de Janeiro.

Another account of Jesuit missionary activity, concerning the Amazon region especially, was by the Jesuit Samuel Fritz (1654-1724) who spent 37 years in the territory. His work was preserved in manuscript at Evora, Portugal. In 1922 the Hakluyt Society at London issued the first English edition as Volume LI of its Second Series. This was a translation from the original Spanish edited by George Edmundson (b. 1848) with the title *Journal of the travels and labours of Father Samuel Fritz in the river of the Amazon between 1686 and 1723.* The account had never before appeared in this complete form, although at Paris in 1781 an abridged French translation had been published.

A military history of the Portuguese colony was written by José de Mirales under the title *Historia militar do Brasil.* It was completed in 1762 but was not published until 1900 when it appeared at Rio de Janeiro. The book covers the period from 1549 to 1762.

2. *Mexico*

Of the histories of New Spain in this century only a few need be named for, as in the case of Brazil, many are of indifferent quality. In 1770 at Mexico City Archbishop Francisco Antonio Lorenzana (1722-1804) published his *Historia de Nueva España* which contained the second, third, and fourth letters of Cortés and other documents of value for the study of the conquest of Mexico.

An earlier work entitled *Teatro americano,* which is statistical in nature, was published at Mexico City in two volumes in 1746. The author was José Antonio de Villa-Señor y Sánchez, the official cosmographer and accountant-general for New Spain, and his writings have been considered very valuable for social and economic facts.

A third and later work, written in Spanish but translated into Italian before publication, was by the Mexican Jesuit and antiquarian, Francisco Javier Clavijero (1731-1787), entitled *Storia antica del Messico,* published at Cesena in 1780 and 1781 in four volumes. The work was illustrated with many maps and plates and is a mine of archæological information. An English translation appeared at London in two volumes in 1787.

A three-volume work treating the early period is the *Historia antigua de México* by Mariano José Fernández de Echeverría y Veytia (1718-1779) which, however, was not published until it appeared at Mexico City in 1836.

A study of great value for the economic historian bears the title *Historia general de real hacienda.* It was written, by order of Viceroy Revillagigedo about 1791, by Fabian de Fonseca (d. 1813) and Carlos de Urrutia. The work appeared in six volumes at Mexico City between 1845 and 1853. It dealt only with New Spain.

A volume dealing with the missionary activities of the Franciscans in New Spain and northern Central America, and containing much useful information concerning the Indians of the same region, is the *Crónica apostólica y seráfica* by Fray Isidro Félix de Espinosa (1679-1755) published at Mexico City in 1746. Another work dealing with the Franciscans is *Chrónica de la provincia de N.S.P. San Francisco de Zacatecas* by José Arlegui, published at Mexico City in 1737. A study dealing with the Franciscans in Michoacán probably was written about 1777 by Pablo de la Purísima Concepión Beaumont, a Franciscan. It was entitled *Crónica de la provincia . . . de Michoacán* and it was first published in five volumes at Mexico City in 1873 and 1874. A new edition in three volumes appeared at the same place in 1932.

A work concerning Jesuit activities appeared in 1754 at Barcelona under the title *Apostólicos afanes de la Compañía de Jesús.* The author is thought to be the Jesuit José de Ortega (1700-1768) and his volume deals with the Jesuits in New Spain and particularly in Pimería Alta.

Another work covering missionary activities was written by Francisco Ximénez (1666-ca. 1722) and bore the title *Historia de la provincia de San Vicente de Chiapa y Guatemala.* It was edited by J. A. Villacorta (b. 1879) in three volumes at Guatemala City, 1929-31. This work should not be confused with one of similar title written early in the seventeenth century by Remesal, to which reference has already been made. The volume edited by Villacorta was based upon a manuscript copy made in the years 1848 to 1875 from an earlier manuscript. The original manuscript is lost.

In 1742 Matías Angel de la Mota Padilla (1688-1766) wrote his *Historia de la conquista de la provincia de la Nueva Galicia* covering the period from 1521 to 1742. The work was printed in two volumes in one at Guadalajara in 1856.

A curious and valuable work in the form of an annual yearbook or *gaceta* which, however, soon suspended publication, appeared at Mexico City between 1728 and 1734. The first three issues appeared under the title *Compendio de noticias mexicanas* (1728-30) and the last four under the title *Compendio de noticias americanas* (1731-34). The author and compiler was Juan Francisco Sahagún de Arévalo. These accounts contained current historical facts from North and South America, the West Indies, and the Philippines and aimed to record valuable material which might otherwise be lost in the archives.

3. *Texas*

The best work of this century dealing with missions and missionaries in Texas (and including New Mexico, California, Northern Mexico, and the Philippines) is the *History of Texas, 1673-1779* by the Franciscan Juan Agustín Morfi (d. 1783) who came to Mexico from Spain about 1755 and after collecting thousands of documents wrote this important account. The manuscript was long lost, but in 1931 C. E. Castañeda of the University of Texas discovered it in Mexico, and in 1935 the Quivira Society published his translation in two volumes at Albuquerque. This work should not be confused with Morfi's *Viaje de Indios y diario de Nueva México* written in 1777 and 1778 and published first at Mexico City in 1856 and brought out in a new edition at the same place in 1936.

4. *Florida*

An excellent work covering Spanish Florida as well as parts of the present United States is by Andrés González Barcia Carballido y Zúñiga entitled *Ensayo cronológico para la historia general de la Florida.* It was published in one volume at Madrid in 1723 and dealt in a comprehensive manner with events between 1512 and 1722.

5. *California*

One of the earliest descriptions of California, and one very valuable for Indian life, is the *Continuación y suplemento a los dos impresos que de orden de este superior givierno han corrido* written by Pedro Fages (d. 1796) and translated into English under the title *A historical, political, and natural description of California* (Berkeley, 1937) by Herbert Ingram Priestley (b. 1875). This translation had first appeared in the *Catholic Historical Review,* January and April, 1919. Fages, an explorer, soldier, amateur ethnologist, and administrator, went on the first expedition to Monterey in 1769. He dated this account November 20, 1775, and it contains two earlier records of the Gálvez expedition: *Extracto de noticias del puerto del Monterrey,* published at Mexico City August 16, 1770; and the *Diario histórica de los viages de mar y tierra hechos al norte de la California,* dated October 24, 1777, and probably published about that time, the author being the engineer Miguel Costansó. Two other works by Fages edited by Priestley are *The Colorado River campaign 1781-1782* (Berkeley, 1913) and the *Expedition to San Francisco in 1770* (Berkeley, 1911).

An interesting and most excellent work dealing with California is that by Miguel Venegas (1680-ca. 1764) entitled *Noticia de la California.* It was published in three volumes at Madrid in 1757, and it deals with the temporal and spiritual conquest of that territory to the middle of the eighteenth century. An English edition was printed at London in two volumes in 1759.

In 1789 at Venice appeared the two volume *Storia della California* by Francisco Javier Clavijero which, like his history of Mexico, was based upon documentary materials and particularly upon the manuscripts of the Jesuits Michael del Barco (1706-1790) and Lucas Ventura, both of whom had lived in the territory. Clavijero's work was translated from the Italian and edited by Sarah E. Lake and A. A. Gray. It was published in 1937 at Stanford University.

The chief account of California missions to 1784 is found in the *Relación histórica de la vida . . . del venerable padre fray Junípero Serra* by Francisco Palóu (1723-89) which was published at Mexico City in 1787. Among the English translations of this work is one which appeared at Santa Barbara in 1934, by Douglas S. Watson (b. 1875). In 1926 Professor Herbert E. Bolton (b. 1870) published at Berkeley in four volumes Palóu's *Historical memoirs of New California.* This work had originally appeared in Spanish under the title *Noticias de la Nueva California* (2 vols., Mexico, 1857), and later in four volumes at San Francisco in 1874.

A volume concerning the region written in this century but not published until the next is the *Historia de la Compañía de Jesús en Nueva España* by Francisco Javier Alegre (1729-1788). It appeared first in three volumes at Mexico City in 1841 and 1842 and was continued by José Mariano Dávila y Arrillaga (1798-1869) in two volumes published at Puebla in 1888 and 1889.

6. *Central America*

Among the volumes dealing with Central America, one in particular should be mentioned. It is the first part of the *Historia de la conquista de la provincia del Itza,* written by an advocate of the Spanish Royal Council, Juan de Villagutierre Soto-Mayor, and it appeared at Madrid in 1701. A second edition appeared at Guatemala City in 1933. No further part of the work has ever been published but even as it is, it constitutes one of the important works dealing with the early history of Yucatan and Guatemala.

A writer who seems to have made considerable use of Remesal's volume on Central America (1619), previously cited, was the Franciscan Francisco Vázquez, who published in two volumes at Guatemala City, 1714-16, the *Crónica de la provincia del santissima nombre de Jesús de Guatemala.* The work was reprinted at Guatemala City in 1937-38.

7. *West Indies*

A work concerning the West Indies which is interesting and frequently used was published in two volumes at London in 1793 under the title *The history of the West Indies,* the author being Bryan Edwards (1743-1809). In 1819 a five-volume augmented edition was published at London. Another excellent historical and descriptive account of the region is contained in *The West-Indies atlas* by Thomas Jefferys, published at London in 1775.

An extensive account of the Island of Haiti based largely upon the manuscript memoir of Jean Baptiste le Pers (1675-1735) was published in four volumes at Amsterdam in 1723 under the title *Histoire de l'île espagnole ou de St. Dominique.* The author was Pierre François Xavier de Charlevoix (1682-1761).

A two-volume work published at Paris in 1776 and 1777 is entitled *Considérations sur l'état présent de la colonie française de Saint-Dominique.* It was by Michel René Hilliard d'Auberteuil (1751-1789).

Another general two-volume work dealing with Santo Domingo bore the title *Description topographique, physique, civile, politique, et historique de la partie française de l'île Saint Dominique. . . .* It was published at Philadelphia during 1797 and 1798, and the author was Médéric Louis Élie Moreau de Saint-Méry (1750-1819).

A brief Spanish work based upon documents collected over a period of twenty years is the *Idea del valor de la isla española* by Antonio Sánchez Valverde (d. 1790). It was published at Madrid in 1785.

8. *Tierra Firme*

Northern South America received attention in a number of histories. In 1723 José de Oviedo y Baños Sotomayor (b. 1674) published at Madrid the first part of his *Historia de la conquista y población de la provincia de Venezuela,* which was written from many early documents (since lost) in the archives at Caracas. It was not until 1885 that the whole work in five volumes appeared at Madrid. However, in 1824 at Caracas an edition was published from which in 1940 at New York was printed a facsimile edition to which were added new illustrations.

In 1741 at Madrid the Jesuit José Gumilla's (1690-ca. 1758) *El Orinoco ilustrado* appeared. This was reissued at Barcelona in two volumes in 1791 under the title *Historia natural, civil y geográfica de las naciones situadas en las riberas del Río Orinoco.* The work was based in part upon facts gleaned during thirty years in the Orinoco region and in part upon the manuscript accounts of Fathers Ribera and Mercado. Another generally descriptive work of value to historians is the *Descripción exacta de la provincia de Venezuela* by José Luis de Cisneros which was published probably at Valencia in 1764. Still another good descriptive work, which includes history and religious activities, is *Cualidades y riquezas del nuevo reino de Granada.* Although written in this century it was not published until it appeared at Bogotá in 1930. The author was Basilio Vicente de Oviedo (b. 1699).

A work entitled *Historia corográfica, natural y evangélica de la Nueva Andalucía . . .* written by the missionary Antonio Caulín (b. 1718) and published at Madrid in 1779, gives many valuable details concerning the natives of northern South America and the activities of the missionaries among them, and also an account of the products of the region.

Another work dealing with the Indians of South America but particularly with those in the Orinoco region is the *Saggio di storia americana* by Felippo Salvadore Gilii, sometimes spelled Gilij, (1721-1789), which was published in four volumes at Rome between 1780 and 1784.

A volume dealing with religious activities in northern South America is the *Historia de las misiones de los llanos* by Juan Rivero (1681-1736), written in 1736 but not published until 1883 when it appeared at Bogotá.

A comprehensive work describing the history, geography, political conditions, etc., of the same locality, as well as of Peru and Chile, was printed at Madrid in 1740 under the title briefly cited *Aviso histórico.* The author was Dionisio de Alcede Ugarte y Herrera (1690-1777). An English edition with many travel accounts added appeared at London in five volumes in 1812. A Spanish edition also with additions was published at Madrid in 1883.

In 1740 there appeared at London a curious work describing this region, together with Cuba, with the title *A geographical description of the coasts, harbours, and sea ports of the Spanish West-Indies.* This had been translated from the manuscript of Domingo González Carranza, "principal pilot of the Flota of New Spain."

9. *Peru*

At Lima, Peru, in 1723 appeared an interesting two-volume history of the founding of that city and of the struggles which immediately followed. The account is in the form of a heroic poem and is entitled briefly *Lima fundada.* The author was Pedro de Peralta Barnuevo Rocha y Benavides (1663-1743), the official cosmographer of Peru, and a scientist and writer of note.

In 1789 an important manuscript was prepared by the Jesuit Juan de Velasco (1727-1819). Two known copies exist at present, both being in Madrid. The title of the manuscript is *La historia del reino de Quito en la América meridional.* It was first published in an incomplete form in two volumes at Paris and Quito in 1837 and 1839. The work may have been based upon a manuscript now lost by Fray Marcos de Niza (ca. 1500-1558) who was in the region before he went to New Spain. In 1840 at Paris Henri Ternaux-Compans edited an incomplete two-volume edition. The most complete edition, however, is that edited by Agustín Yerovi (d. 1903) which appeared at Quito in three volumes between 1841 and 1844. This work bears the title *Historia del reino de Quito,* and deals with the ancient history of Ecuador to the time of the Spanish conquest, which the author divides into three periods.

A work of great value for the historian of the later colonial period in Peru is the five-volume *Guía política, eclesiástica y militar del virreynato del*

Perú by José Hipólito Unánue (1755-1833). The work appeared at Lima between 1793 and 1797 and covered the same years in the form of an annual publication.

10. La Plata

A volume describing the Gran Chaco was published at Córdoba, Argentina, in 1733, under the title *Descripción corográfica.* The author was Pedro Lozano and his account, which is the earliest of the region, is very comprehensive and includes much history and biography as well as geography. The same author wrote an account of the conquest of southern South America under the title *Historia de la conquista del Paraguay, Río de la Plata y Tucumán.* This work, however, was not published until it appeared in five volumes at Buenos Aires between 1873 and 1875.

A history of Paraguay frequently cited is that by Pierre François Xavier de Charlevoix entitled *Histoire du Paraguay,* published at Paris in three volumes in 1756 and 1757. It has been translated into many languages including English (2 vols., Dublin, 1769).

A valuable historical and ethnological work on Paraguay written in this century but not published until 1910 in two volumes at Buenos Aires is *El Paraguay católico* by the Jesuit José Sánchez Labrador (b. 1717).

A German work entitled *Geschichte von Paraguay* by Bernard Nusdorfer was published at Frankfurt in 1769. This book dealt largely with the activities of the Jesuits in the territory.

Argentina and the neighboring regions are described in two accounts by the missionaries, Thomas Falkner (1707-1784), a Jesuit, who lived among the Patagonian Indians from 1740 to 1767, in his *Description of Patagonia and the adjoining parts of South America* published at Hereford in 1774 and reprinted at Chicago in 1935; and Martin Dobritzhofer (1717-1791) in his three-volume *Historia de Abiponibus,* published at Vienna in 1784. An English edition of this latter work appeared at London in three volumes in 1822. This is in part a memoir of eighteen years among the natives, and it constitutes one of the most extraordinary descriptions of savage life ever published. Dobritzhofer entered the Jesuit Order in 1736 and went to South America as a missionary in 1749, spending many years among the Indians.

11. Chile

One of the chief eighteenth century works concerning Chile was written in Italian by the Chilean Jesuit Juan Ignacio Molina (ca. 1737-1829) under the title *Saggio sulla storia naturale del Chili* and was published at Bologna in 1782. For some time after the book appeared it was generally believed to be the work of Felipe Gómez de Vidaurre (b. 1740). In 1787 the second part of the work appeared at Bologna under the title *Saggio sulla storia civile del Chili.* The first English edition of Molina's account was printed in two volumes at Middletown, Connecticut, in 1808, and the next year a two-volume edition appeared at London. An earlier anonymous work by the same author had been published at Bologna in 1776 under the title *Compendio della storia, geografica, naturale e civile del regno del Chili.* This was printed in Spanish at Madrid in two volumes between 1788 and 1795. Another Spanish edition was published in *Colección de historiadores de Chile,* at Santiago, as volumes XI (1878) and XXVI (1901).

An interesting descriptive work dealing with Chile, and also Peru, was written by Amédée François Frézier (1682-1773) who was sent by the French king Louis XIV to investigate the country. The book is entitled *Relation du voyage de la Mer du Sud aux côtes de Chily et du Perou, 1712-13-14,* and it appeared first at Paris in 1716. The first English edition was printed at London in 1717. A Spanish translation of part of the work appeared at Santiago in 1902.

Another work concerning Chile which appeared toward the end of the century is briefly cited as *Chilidugu.* It was written by the Jesuit missionary, Bernardi Havestadt (ca. 1708-1781), and was printed in Latin in two volumes in Westphalia in 1777.

CHAPTER FOUR

NINETEENTH CENTURY WORKS

A. Introduction

B. General works
   1. History, geography, description, etc.
   2. Anthropology, archaeology, ethnology, etc.
   3. Discovery, conquest, colonization, etc.
   4. Revolutions for independence
   5. Voyages and travels

C. Works on individual countries and regions
   1. Brazil
   2. Mexico
   3. Central America (Guatemala)
   4. Honduras
   5. Nicaragua
   6. Costa Rica
   7. West Indies
   8. Cuba
   9. Santo Domingo and Haiti
   10. Puerto Rico
   11. Colombia
   12. Venezuela
   13. Ecuador
   14. Peru
   15. Bolivia
   16. Paraguay
   17. Argentina
   18. Uruguay
   19. Chile

A. INTRODUCTION

The nineteenth century, which was disturbed by nationalism, imperialism, and industrialism, saw many works produced dealing in general with Hispanic America. At the beginning of the century Hispanic America succeeded in breaking away from the deadening influence of the mother countries and in winning independence. The consequent disturbances in America and the concurrent disturbances in Europe resulting from the activities of Napoleon and Metternich brought new interest in democracy to the peoples of America, while the Monroe Doctrine concentrated attention upon the Western Hemisphere. With the rise of dictators in Hispanic America party rivalry and political struggles tended to continue to attract the attention of European nations. All of these circumstances produced in literature partisan accounts and controversial histories, and at the same time stimulated travel by European visitors who published the records of their experiences. Yet in this century German dilettantism had its influence upon historical production, and even in Hispanic America the hypercritical historian found material for his pen, as did the more robust and dependable scholarly writer of erudite history. Of the vast number of historical works of this century dealing wholly or in part with these countries, only a few outstanding examples are here given.

B. General Works

1. *History, Geography, Description, etc.*

One of the most extensive of the general histories of this century was that by Giuseppe Compagnoni (1754-1833), who, continuing the work of the Conte di Segur (1756-1805), published the *Storia dell' America* in twenty-nine volumes at Milan in 1820.

In 1823 the first of the four-volume *Geografía general* edited by Feliciano Montenegro Colón (d.1853) appeared at Caracas. The last volume was published in 1837. Taken as a whole, this work, despite its name, is more historical than geographical.

An extensive compilation on maritime law appeared at Paris in six volumes between 1828 and 1845 of which Volume VI dealt with Spain and Portugal. The work was written by Jean Marie Pardessus (1772-1853) and bore the title *Collection de lois maritimes antérieures au XVIIIe siècle.*

Between 1864 and 1866 Gil Gelpi y Ferro (1826-1894) published at Havana his two-volume *Estudios sobre la América.* Meanwhile, in 1865 at Santiago, Chile, appeared the *Compendio de historia de América* in two volumes by the justly famous Diego Barros Arana (1830-1907). In 1913 at Buenos Aires this work appeared in a new brief edition in one volume under the title *Compendio elemental de historia de América.*

In 1875 Miguel Lobo y Malagamba (d.1876) brought out in three volumes at Madrid his *Historia general de las antiguas colonias hispano-americanas.* Two years later in 1877 at Caracas was published the *Biografías de hombres notables de Hispano-América* in four volumes written by Ramón Azpurúa. This work is of particular value to the historian of the independence period.

Another work of great value to historians, and one which contains many early relations of a descriptive and geographic nature largely dealing with Peru, was published by the Ministerio de Fomento of Peru in four volumes at Madrid between 1881 and 1897 under the title *Relaciones geográficas de indias.*

In 1883 there appeared at Bogotá the *Biografía de hombres ilustres* by Soledad Acosta de Samper (1833-1913), a woman novelist and editor. This work was used as a historical textbook in Colombian schools. In 1888 Adolfo Flórez (d.1895) published at the same place his one-volume *Estudio cronológico*. The same year at Barcelona appeared the first part of the *Historia general de América desde sus tiempos más remotos* (two volumes in one). The author, Francisco Pi y Margall (1824-1901), was a lawyer and newspaperman. He never completed his work, which was written at the request of a Madrid publishing company. The study deals with pre-Columbian history. An earlier, preliminary edition appeared in 1878.

From 1889 to 1897 Ricardo Cappa (1800-1897) published at Madrid his extensive *Estudios críticos acerca de la dominación española en América* in twenty volumes, the first part of which had appeared at Madrid a few years before. While this work was being published there appeared in 1892 at Barcelona the excellent and well-illustrated three-volume *América* by Rodolfo Cronau (b.1855), covering the period from the earliest times but placing most emphasis upon the age of discoveries. During 1894 and 1895 the *América* of José Coroleu é Inglada (1840-1895) appeared in four volumes at Barcelona covering the whole scope of Hispanic American history.

Among general French works written in this century one of the earliest to treat Hispanic America was that by Alexander von Humboldt (1769-1859), who, with Aimé Jacques Alexandre Bonpland (1773-1858), traveled through South America between the years 1799 and 1804. Their works were published in twenty-three volumes between 1805 and 1834. Sections of these volumes have been reprinted at various times, and between 1836 and 1839 at Paris five volumes were reprinted under the title *Examen critique de l'histoire de la géographie du nouveau continent* and contained considerable valuable information for historians. This work had been preceded by an account translated into English in seven volumes (London, 1814-29) entitled *Personal narrative of travels to the equinoctial regions of the new continent, during the years 1799-1804.*

From 1835 to 1847 there appeared in French at Paris the nine-volume work by the naturalist Alcide Dessalines d'Orbigny (1802-1857) and entitled *Voyage dans l'Amérique méridionale . . .* (during the years 1826 to 1833). The region covered embraced Brazil, Argentina, Uruguay, Chile, Bolivia, and Peru. The same author edited and published at Paris in 1836 his *Voyage pittoresque dans les deux Amériques . . .*, which was translated and revised for publication in Spanish under the title *Viaje pintoresco a las dos Américas, Asia y Africa . . .* (3 vols., Barcelona, 1842). This is a general survey of voyages of discovery from the time of Columbus.

Between 1875 and 1894 Jean Jacques Élisée Reclus (1830-1905) brought out at Paris his *Nouvelle géographie universelle* in nineteen volumes, of which Volumes XV to XIX treated the geography and history of America. From 1890 to 1893 an English edition in three volumes containing the material on North America was published at New York, while during 1894 and 1895 two volumes dealing with South America appeared at the same place. All of these volumes were edited by Augustus Henry Keane (1833-1912) and given the title *The earth and its inhabitants.*

In 1876 at Paris appeared the *Histoire de l'Amérique du Sud* by Alfred Joseph Deberle (1835-1877). The third French edition (1897) was translated into English and published at London in 1899. This work dealt with Hispanic America from the time of the conquest. In 1932 a new edition of this book was published at New York. In 1882 at Paris appeared *Les états latins de l'Amérique* by Adalbert Frout de Fontpertuis (b.1825).

Among German works dealing in general with Hispanic America, one of the earliest was the three-volume *Amerika* by Franz Jakob Kutscher (d.1821), published at Schleswig in 1803, which was concerned largely with the natives of Spanish America. Another German work was published at Frankfurt am Main in two volumes in 1850. It was entitled *Geschichte der colonisation Amerika's* by Franz Justus Kottenkamp (1806-1858). In 1885 at Leipzig appeared the third edition of Wilhelm Georg Friedrich Roscher's (1817-1894) *Kolonien* . . . which contained an excellent sketch of the Spanish colonies in America. This discussion was translated and edited by E. G. Bourne (1860-1908) under the title *The Spanish colonial system* (New York, 1904). This little study is doubtless the best brief statement concerning the subject in the English language.

A Dutch work of description and travel published in two volumes at Amsterdam in 1828 bore the title *Beschrijving der niewe staten van Amerika.* The author was Johann Gottfried Sommer (ca.1782-1848).

A comparatively large number of general histories or near-histories of Hispanic America were published in English in the nineteenth century. In 1808 Abeil Holmes (1763-1837) published at Cambridge, Massachusetts, for the first time *The annals of America* in two volumes, which constituted a concise work containing much useful information. The volumes were reprinted subsequently in both England and America.

In 1818 at London appeared Sir Richard Henry Bonnycastle's (1791-1848) *Spanish America* in two volumes. The first volume dealt with Spanish North America and New Granada, and the second volume treated the remainder of Spanish America. The work is descriptive, geographical, and historical.

In 1823 H. C. Carey (1793-1879) and I. Lea (1792-1886) published at Philadelphia and London *The geography, history, and statistics of America and the West Indies;* and in 1825 at New York the two-volume work by John Milton Niles (1787-1856) appeared under the title *A view of South America and Mexico.*

In the decade of the forties two useful works appeared. One, of limited historical value, was Charles Darwin's (1809-1882) *Geological observations* published in three parts at London between 1842 and 1846 and later republished in Spanish at Santiago, Chile, in 1906. The other study was brought out in 1848 by Samuel G. Goodrich (1793-1860) at Louisville under the title *History of South America and the West Indies.*

From 1856 to 1868 Sir Arthur Helps (1813-1875) published at New York his four-volume work entitled *The Spanish conquest in America.* This had been preceded by *The conquerors of the new world and their bondsmen* (2 vols., London, 1848-52), treating of the enslavement of the Negroes in the West Indies and on the mainland.

In 1877 E. J. Payne (1844-1904) published at London his volume on the *History of European colonies,* which was followed by two volumes entitled the *History of the new world called America* (Oxford, 1892-99). This work, however, was never finished and in consequence did not get beyond the treatment of aboriginal America.

In 1878 at London Henry W. Bates (1825-1892) edited a volume entitled *Central America and the West Indies and South America.* This work had been translated by A. H. Keane from the German and is sometimes referred to as *Stanford's compendium of geography and travel.* The original work upon which these volumes are based is Friedrich Anton Heller von Hellwald's (1842-1892) *Die erde und ihre völker* (2 vols., Stuttgart, 1877-78).

In 1880 appeared the first edition of Antonio Carlo Napoleone's *South America,* which was published at London. In 1884 R. G. Watson published at the same place his two-volume *Spanish and Portuguese South America during the colonial period.* Between 1884 and 1889 at Boston was published Justin Winsor's (1831-1897) co-operative and monumental *Narrative and critical history of America* in eight volumes, which dealt at some length with Hispanic America.

In 1891 Theodore Childs brought out at New York *The Spanish American republics,* which was also published the same year in French at Paris. In 1893 Charles F. Lummis published at Chicago his excellent little volume on *The Spanish pioneers,* while in the same year in New York appeared a work of somewhat similar nature by the historian, archaeologist, and ethnologist, Adolph Francis Alphonse Bandelier (1840-1914), entitled *The Gilded Man (El Dorado) and other pictures of Spanish occupancy in America.* In 1898 Hezekiah Butterworth (1839-1905) published at New York his *South America,* which dealt largely with the independence movement, and in 1900 at Akron, Ohio, appeared a volume entitled *South America* by F. G. Carpenter (1855-1924), which described society, politics, economic life, and so on.

2. *Anthropology, Archaeology, Ethnology, etc.*

General histories on special topics are numerous. Among the volumes dealing with the American natives written in this century, several are worthy of note. In 1878 and 1879 appeared *Die culturländer des alten Amerika* by Philip Wilhelm Adolf Bastian (1826-1905). Its three volumes were published in two at Berlin.

In 1810 the beautiful and excellent *Vues des cordillères, et monuments des peuples indigènes de l'Amérique,* by Alexander von Humboldt, was published at Paris. Four years later this appeared at London in a two-volume English translation entitled *Researches concerning the institutions and monuments of the ancient inhabitants of America.*

Another important volume dealing with native cultures is *L'Amérique préhistorique* by Jean François Albert du Pouget, Marquis de Nadaillac (b.1818), published at Paris in 1883. This was translated into English and printed at London in 1885 under the title *Prehistoric America.*

A still indispensable work, which appeared at London in nine volumes (1830-48), is the *Antiquities of Mexico* by Lord Kingsborough (1795-1837). It is illustrated by more than 1,000 plates, many of them colored, showing early Mexican picture writing, architecture, and art, and it constitutes a mine of archaeological information.

Another work dealing with early Mexican art and archaeology is the *Monumentos del arte mexicano antiguo* by Antonio Peñafiel (b.1831), published in three volumes (one volume text and two volumes portfolio) at Berlin in 1890. The illustrations are handsomely done.

Still another important contribution to this subject is the *Histoire des nations civilisées du Mexique et de l'Amérique Centrale* by the Abbé Charles-Étienne Brasseur de Bourbourg (1814-1874), published at Paris in four volumes between 1857 and 1859. The work is based upon an immense amount of research and deals with native cultures before the time of Columbus.

A brief English volume frequently cited is *The American race* by Daniel G. Brinton (1837-1899), published at New York in 1891, which describes the linguistic and ethnological characteristics of the Indians of North and South America.

Two brief works of limited value to the student of Hispanic America are George Catlin's (1796-1872) *Letters and notes on the manners, customs, and conditions of the North American Indians,* published in two volumes at London in 1841; and Thomas Francis Gordon's (1787-1860) *The history of America,* published in two volumes at Philadelphia in 1831, which carries the story only as far as the destruction of the Aztec empire. In 1832 at Philadelphia appeared two more volumes with the title *The history of Mexico* covering the same period and based chiefly on Javier Clavijero's (1731-1787) *Storia Antica del Messico* (4 vols., Cesena, 1780-81).

One of the most elaborate works from the standpoint of illustrations is that by Johann Wilhelm Reiss (1838-1908) and Alfons Stübel (1835-1904) entitled *The necropolis of Ancón* (in Peru) which was published in English at Berlin in three volumes between 1880 and 1887. Another elaborate and classic work dealing with the highland civilization of the Peruvian coast is *Die ruinenstaette von Tiahuanaco* by Alfons Stübel and Friedrich Max Uhle (b.1856). This was published at Leipzig in two parts in 1892.

In 1889 and 1890 a two-volume work of extreme value to the student of the South American Indian, and particularly of the Peruvian Indian, was issued at Berlin. It was entitled *Kultur und industrie Südamerikanischer völker* and was the work of Friedrich Max Uhle in collaboration with Alfons Stübel, Johann Wilhelm Reiss, and P. Koppell.

Two other works dealing with Incan life should be consulted by all interested in the subject. The first is *Antigüedades peruanas* (one volume and atlas, Vienna, 1851) by Johann Jakob von Tschudi (1818-1889) and Mariano Eduardo de Ribero y Ustáriz (1795-1857). This work was translated into English and published at New York in 1853 under the title *Peruvian antiquities.* New editions appeared at the same place in 1854 and 1855. The second study is also by Tschudi. It bears the title *Culturhistorische und sprachliche beiträge zur kenntniss des alten Peru* (Wien, 1891). A two-volume Spanish translation appeared at Lima in 1918 entitled *Contribuciones a la historia, civilización y lingüística del Perú antiguo.*

3. *Discovery, Conquest, Colonization, etc.*

On the discovery period several books should be mentioned. In 1892 at Boston, Massachusetts, John Fiske (1842-1901) published *The discovery of America* in two volumes. While not always accurate, this has been considered one of the chief guides to the subject in English. A book of value written in Spanish is *Historia del descubrimiento de América* (Madrid, 1893) by Emilio Castelar y Ripoll (1832-1899).

The volumes of Henry Harrisse (1830-1910), *Les Corte-Real et leurs voyages au nouveau-monde* (2 vols., Paris, 1883), *Americus Vespuccius* (London, 1895), *Fernand Colomb, sa vie, ses oeuvres* (Paris, 1872), *Christophe Colomb* (2 vols., Paris, 1884-85), and *The discovery of North America* (London, 1892), the latter an admirable cartographical essay, are all of value to the student of this period.

In 1828 Washington Irving (1783-1859) brought out at London and New York his four-volume *History of the life and voyages of Christopher Columbus,* which soon after was translated into most European languages.

The greatest work dealing with Columbus and the period of discoveries in any language is the *Raccolta di documenti e studi* published in fifteen volumes by the Italian government at Rome between 1892 and 1894. This work is, however, very scarce, as the edition was limited to 560 sets.

Although only thirty pages in length, a scholarly and valuable study of the Portuguese discoverers and their explorations before the time of Columbus is the very brief *Navegaciones y descubrimientos de los portugueses* written by Joaquim Pedro Oliveira Martins (1845-1894) and published at Madrid in 1892. A work more familiar to American students is *The golden age of Prince Henry the navigator,* translated from his *Os fihos de D. João I* and printed at London in 1914.

An account of the discovery of America by the Norsemen was printed in a collection of documents in Dutch at Hafniae (i.e., Copenhagen) in 1837 under the title *Antiquitates Americanae sive scriptores septentrionales rerum ante-Columbianarum in America.* In 1839 there appeared in English at London another work on the Norse discoveries entitled *The discovery of America by the Norsemen* which aimed to prove the truth of the claims. The author was Joshua Toulmin Smith (1816-1869), who brought out at Boston in the same year the same volume with the title *The Northmen in New England.*

A volume dealing with Negro slavery in America is entitled *Historia de la esclavitud de la raza africana en el nuevo mundo y en especial en los países américo-hispanos* (Barcelona, 1879). The author was José Antonio Saco (1797-1879), and this book is generally considered a supplement to his history of slavery published at Paris in three volumes between 1875 and 1877. A new edition was printed at Havana in two volumes in 1932 with an introduction by Fernando Ortiz (b.1881); in 1938 the work was reissued in four volumes at Havana.

4. *Revolutions for Independence*

General works dealing with the independence period and with military matters are numerous. Between 1864 and 1867 at Paris appeared the *Annales historiques de la révolution de l'Amérique latine* in five volumes written by the famous internationalist, Carlos Calvo (1824-1906). The text, in Spanish, covers the period from 1808. At the same time appeared the author's *Recueil complet des traités . . . ,* published at Paris in eleven volumes between 1862 and 1869. Another but earlier work published at Paris was by Pierre Joseph Spiridion Dufey (1770-1854) entitled *Résumé de l'histoire des révolutions de l'Amérique méridionale.* It was printed in two volumes in 1826.

In 1858 and 1859 Bartolomé Mitre (1821-1906) brought out at Buenos Aires the first two volumes of his *Historia de Belgrano y la independencia argentina.* A third volume was added in 1876 and the work was published in four volumes in 1902. In 1890 was published the first edition of his *Historia de San Martín y de la emancipación de Sud-América* at Buenos Aires in four volumes. This was partly translated into English by William Pilling and published at London in 1893 in one volume under the title *The emancipation of South America.*

A work dealing with the independence period from the Spanish point of view was written at the command of Fernando VII and published at Madrid in three volumes in 1829 and 1830. It was entitled *Historia de la revolución hispano-americana* and the author was Mariano Torrente (1792-1856). Parts of the work dealing especially with the independence movements in Chile and in Mexico have been republished under various titles.

Another Spanish work bears the title *Las glorias nacionales* and was written by Fernando Patxot y Ferrer (1812-1859) to show the relations between Spain and Spanish America. The work was published in six volumes at Barcelona between 1852 and 1854.

5. *Voyages and Travels*

As in the eighteenth century, collections of voyages and travels are numerous and frequently constitute valuable sources of historical information. Among the most important of such works the following should be mentioned in the order of their appearance.

Between 1803 and 1817 there began to appear at London a carefully compiled five-volume work entitled *A chronological history of the discoveries in the South Sea or Pacific Ocean*. The author was James Burney (1750-1821), a careful compiler. The first volume dealt with the period to 1579; Volume II (published in 1806) continued the story to 1620; Volume III (1813) treated the years 1620-88; Volume IV (1816) covered the years 1688-1723; and Volume V (1817) carried the work to 1764. These volumes are very useful for the student of early California history and for discoveries in the Pacific.

Meanwhile, at Paris in 1808 appeared in six volumes another work of considerable value to the historian of the discovery period under the title *Bibliothèque universelle des voyages*, of which part five is devoted to America. The author was Gilles Boucher de la Richarderie (1733-1810).

From 1808 to 1814 at London appeared seventeen volumes under the title *A general collection of the best and most interesting voyages and travels in all parts of the world*. The editor, who was John Pinkerton (1758-1826), put into this collection the accounts of a number of early voyages hitherto unpublished in English.

From 1811 to 1824 Robert Kerr's *General history and collection of voyages and travels* appeared at Edinburgh in eighteen volumes, the last volume of which contained a bibliography of voyages and travels compiled by W. Stevenson.

Between 1825 and 1837 there appeared at Madrid the five-volume *Colección de los viages y descubrimientos que hicieron por mar los españoles desde fines del siglo XV* by Martín Fernández de Navarrete (1765-1844). This included various documents concerning Columbus, Vespucci, Magellan, and others, and dealt with the Spanish establishments in America. The work was never completed because of the compiler's death.

In 1833 there began to appear at Paris the *Bibliothèque universelle des voyages par mer ou par terre dans les divers parties du monde* which covered the period from the earliest times. The work was completed in forty-six volumes, together with an atlas published in 1837. The editor was Albert Montemont (1788-1861).

In this latter year (1837) there was published at Paris the first of a series of ten volumes entitled *Voyages, relations, et mémoires originaux pour servir à l'histoire de la découverte de l'Amérique.* In 1840 appeared ten more volumes at Paris. The editor was Henri Ternaux-Compans, and the collection contained many Spanish accounts written before 1700, some of which were translated from the Spanish manuscripts and all of which were published for the first time in French.

The greatest project of the nineteenth century in the realm of collecting, editing, and translating earlier accounts was undertaken by the Hakluyt Society, which in 1847 began to issue its first series of voyages and travels in one hundred volumes (London, 1847-98). A second series of eighty-five volumes (London, 1899-1940) continued the admirable work begun in the first series.

C. Works on Individual Countries and Regions

Histories dealing with specific portions of Hispanic America became increasingly numerous during the nineteenth century as each state won and maintained its individual freedom.

1. *Brazil*

The independence of Brazil and its vicissitudes during the period of the empire and the early republic attracted the attention of writers in many countries. In 1808 Andrew Grant published his *History of Brazil* at London, which was intended not only as a history but as a guide for those who contemplated a journey to that country.

In 1810 the first volume of Robert Southey's (1774-1843) well-known *History of Brazil* was published at London. The second volume appeared in 1817, and the third and last in 1819.

Meanwhile, in 1815 there appeared at Paris the comprehensive three-volume *Histoire du Brésil* by Alphonse de Beauchamps (1767-1832), covering the years from 1500 to 1810, which Robert Southey said was copied chiefly from Volume I of his *History of Brazil;* in 1817 appeared the *Corografia basilica* (two volumes at Rio de Janeiro) by the churchman Manuel Ayres de Casal (b.ca.1754) from which James Henderson (ca.1783-1848) compiled his *History of Brazil* (1 vol., London, 1821); and in 1819 at Frankfurt was published the valuable two-volume *Reise nach Brasilien* during the years 1815, 1816, and 1817, by Maximilian, Prinz zu Wied-Neuwied (1782-1867). The first volume of the latter work was translated into English and published at London in 1820.

In 1821 a Frenchman, Jean Ferdinand Denis (1798-1890), published at Paris his history and travel account, *Le Brésil.* Eight years later, in 1829, at Dresden appeared the *Geschichte von Brasilien* in two volumes by Ernst Münch (1798-1841). Between 1826 and 1830 appeared in four parts the incomplete *Historia dos principaes successos politicos do imperio do Brasil* by José da Silva Lisbôa, who was commissioned by Dom Pedro I to write the official history of the independence movement. Meanwhile there appeared in three volumes (München, 1823-31) the valuable *Reise in Brasilien,* covering the years 1817 to 1820, by Johann Baptiste von Spix (1781-1826) and Carl Friedrich Philipp von Martius (1794-1868). A Portuguese translation of this work was printed at Rio de Janeiro in two volumes in 1938.

An extensive work in four volumes which dealt with the Province of Bahia and which was written by Ignacio Accioli de Cerqueira e Silva was published at the city of Bahia in 1835. It bore the title *Memorias historicas e politicas.*

In 1836 John Armitage (1807-1856) published at London his two-volume *History of Brazil* which was intended to be a continuation of Southey's work and carried the story from 1808 to 1831. In 1839 Francisco Solano Constancia (1777-1846) brought out his *Historia do Brasil* at Paris in two volumes, which traced the history of the country from the earliest times to the abdication of Dom Pedro I.

Between 1842 and 1876 appeared at Paris eighteen volumes published in thirteen the *Quadro elementar das relações politicas e diplomaticas de Portugal* by Manoel Francisco de Barros, Visconde de Santarem (1791-1856). The work is indispensable to the student of the external relations of Brazil. From 1842 to 1853 at Paris appeared from the pen of the same writer his *Atlas* . . . , which is the chief source for the study of Portuguese colonial expansion.

In 1843 the two-volume work of the revolutionary and adventurer, José Ignacio de Abreu e Lima (1796-1869), appeared at Rio de Janeiro under the title *Compendio da historia do Brasil.* This was followed at Pernambuco two years later by his *Synopsis* containing the chief facts in Brazilian history.

Between 1854 and 1857 Francisco Adolpho de Varnhagen, the great authority on the colonial period, brought out his comprehensive *Historia geral do Brasil* in two volumes at Rio de Janeiro. This was followed in 1871 at Vienna by his *Historia das lutas com os Hollandezes no Brasil desde 1624 a 1654.* He is also the author of a number of other works of a more special nature. The latest edition of his general history appeared at São Paulo in five volumes in 1936.

In 1857 Daniel P. Kidder (1815-1891) and James C. Fletcher published at Boston their profusely illustrated *Brazil and the Brazilians,* describing the country and its people and summarizing its history. In 1860 at Berlin was published the large one-volume *Geschichte von Brasilien* by Heinrich Handelmann (1827-1891). This work was translated into Portuguese and issued at Rio de Janeiro in 1931 under the contracted title *Historia do Brasil.* . . . Between 1864 and 1868 appeared at Rio de Janeiro the monumental seven-volume *Historia da fundação do imperio brasileiro* by João Manoel Pereira da Silva (ca.1819-1898), who was the author of numerous other extremely valuable works on the same period. Meanwhile, in 1866 at London, William Scully, the editor of the *Anglo-Brazilian Times,* brought out a handbook of useful information on the country entitled briefly *Brazil.* In this connection should be mentioned a source of great help to the student of diplomatic history entitled *Apontamentos para o direito internacional* . . . (4 vols., Rio de Janeiro, 1864-69), edited by Antonio Pereira Pinto (1819-1880).

From 1871 to 1873 there appeared at Rio de Janeiro the two-volume *Historia do Brazil* . . . by Alexandre José de Mello Moraes (1816-1882), which covered the period between 1808 and 1871. This work had been preceded at Rio de Janeiro from 1858 to 1863 by the five-volume *Corographia historica . . . do imperio do Brasil.*

At Rio de Janeiro in 1871 appeared the *Guerra do Paraguay* by Emilio Carlos Jourdan, which discusses Brazil's conflict with that state.

In 1889 at Rio de Janeiro was printed the very useful *Historia financeira e orçamentaria do imperio do Brasil desde sua fundação* by Liberato de Castro Carreira (b.1820). In the same year at Paris was published *Dom Pedro II, empereur du Brésil,* written by Benjamin Mossé (b.1832).

In 1894 appeared at Rio de Janeiro the naval history of the Paraguayan War compiled from the documents by Affonso Celso de Assis Figueiredo, Visconde de Ouro Preto (1836-1912), under the title *A marinha d'outr'ora.* . . .

In 1894 and 1895 the *Historia constitucional da republica dos Estados Unidos do Brasil* by Felisbello Firmo de Oliveira Freire (b.1858) was published in three volumes at Rio de Janeiro. It deals with the transition from empire to republic. In 1896 Joaquim Francisco de Assis Brasil (1857-1938) brought out his *Do governo presidencial na republica brasileira* at Lisbon. In the same year at São Paulo was published the two-volume *Compendio de historia do Brasil* by Raphael Maria Galanti (b.1840). In 1899 at Rio de Janeiro Benjamín Franklin de Ramiz Galvão (1846-1938) issued his *Galeria de historia brazileira, 1500-1900.*

Between 1898 and 1900 there appeared at Lisbon two volumes entitled *Trabalhos nauticos dos Portuguezes nos seculos XVI e XVII,* written by Francisco Marques de Sousa Viterbo (1845-1910). In 1899 at Leipzig appeared the comprehensive one-volume *Brasilien* by Oskar Constatt (b.1842), and in 1900 an advanced textbook entitled *Historia do Brasil* was published at Rio de Janeiro by João Baptista Ribeiro de Andrada Fernandes (1860-1934).

2. *Mexico*

Histories dealing with Mexico in this century were very numerous and of considerable value. In 1811 there appeared at Paris the five volumes of Alexander von Humboldt entitled *Essai politique sur le royaume de la Nouvelle Espagne* which had first been published as Part III of the *Voyage de Humboldt et Bonpland* (23 vols., Paris, 1805-34). A Spanish edition appeared at Paris in 1822 in five volumes, and an English edition was printed at London in four volumes in 1811. Because of the extreme value of this work most subsequent writers on Mexico have found it necessary to refer to it.

In 1813 at London appeared the two-volume *Historia de la revolución de Nueva España* by José Servando Teresa Mier Noriega y Guerra (1765-1827).

Between 1821 and 1823 at Rio de Janeiro was printed the two-volume *Historia do descubrimento e conquista do imperio mexicano* by Antonio Vicente Dellanave. Between the latter year and 1832 there appeared at Mexico City the six-volume *Cuadro histórico de la revolución de la América mexicana* by Carlos María de Bustamante (1774-1848). This work was written in the form of letters from 1823 to 1832. In 1824 Nicholas Mill's *History of Mexico* was published at London, covering the period from the earliest times and dealing with all phases of national life, but particularly stressing the mineral wealth of the country which the author hoped British capital would exploit.

In 1831 and 1832 appeared at Paris and New York the first edition of Lorenzo de Zavala's (1788-1836) two-volume *Ensayo histórico de las revoluciones de México desde 1808 hasta 1830.* A new edition was printed in two volumes at Mexico City in 1918. In 1836 *Méjico y sus revoluciones* by José María Luis Mora (1794-1850) was published at Paris in three volumes. Between 1836 and 1838 the four-volume work by Andrés Cavo (b.1739) entitled *Los tres siglos de México durante el gobierno español* was printed at Mexico City.

In 1843 appeared the first edition of William H. Prescott's classic *History of the conquest of Mexico* in three volumes at New York. This was followed the next year by an edition published at London.

Between 1844 and 1849 there appeared at Mexico City a three-volume work by Lucas Alamán (1792-1853) which bore the title *Disertaciones sobre la historia de la república mexicana.* This was followed at Mexico City between 1849 and 1852 by his five-volume *Historia de Méjico* covering the period since 1808.

In 1852 and 1853 appeared Brantz Mayer's (1809-1879) *Mexico,* a historical descriptive work dealing with the whole field of Mexican history. It was published in two volumes at Hartford, Connecticut. In 1862 Francisco Carbajal Espinosa brought out his *Historia de México* (2 vols., Mexico) which covered the history of the country from the earliest times to the middle of the nineteenth century.

An important work for the historian appeared at Mexico City in two volumes (1862-65) under the title *Cuadro descriptivo y comparativo de las lenguas indígenas de México.* The author was Francisco Pimentel (1832-1893). Another valuable work by the same author (Mexico, 1883) bore the title *Historia crítica de la literatura y de las ciencias en México desde la conquista hasta nuestros días.* This work, however, which was never completed, included only poetry.

A work reprinted in several languages appeared in 1863 at Paris under the title *Le Mexique, ancien et moderne.* The author was Michel Chevalier (1806-1879). A two-volume English edition was published at London in 1864, and a one-volume Spanish edition appeared at Madrid two years later (1866).

An extensive work in six volumes by Ignacio Alvarez (1833-1904) entitled *Estudios sobre la historia general de México* was published at Zacatecas from 1869 to 1877. An even more detailed study, although only in four volumes, was published at Madrid in 1871 and 1872. It was entitled *Méjico desde 1808 á 1867,* and the author was Francisco de Paula de Arrangois y Berzábal (d.1889).

The first four volumes of a reference work which, however, was never completed was published at Mexico City in 1874 and 1875 under the title *Diccionario geográfico, estadístico, histórico, biográfico, . . .* The author was José María Pérez Hernández, and the volumes covered the letters A to C only. Another special work of historical value is entitled *México pintoresco, artístico y monumental* by Manuel Rivera Cambas and published at Mexico City in 1880. This had been preceded by his two-volume work entitled *Los governantes de México,* published at Mexico City in 1872 and 1873.

In 1880 at Mexico City was published, four volumes in two, the *Historia antigua y de la conquista de México* by the historian and geographer Manuel Orozco y Berra (1816-1881). The next year at the same place appeared his *Apuntes para la historia de la geografía en México.* Many other works have appeared from this scholar's pen, including the four-volume *Historia de la dominación española en México* written in 1849 but not published until it appeared at Mexico City in 1938.

In 1883 at Guadalajara appeared the *Compendio de la historia de México* by Luis Pérez Verdía. Between 1884 and 1888 appeared at Lagos a three-volume essay, briefly entitled *Principios críticos* by Agustín Rivera y Sanromán (1824-1916), which dealt largely with the colonial and revolutionary periods. From 1888 to 1891 at Mexico City was published the valuable five-volume *Diccionario geográfico, histórico y biográfico de los estados unidos mexicanos,* the work of Antonio García Cubas (b.1832).

Two valuable works of a special nature appearing in the decade of the eighties were the *Historia de la medicina en México desde la época de los indios hasta la presente* (3 vols., Mexico, 1886-88) by Francisco A. Flores, and the *Geografía y estadística de la república mexicana* (12 vols., Mexico, 1889-92) by Alfonso Luis Velasco.

In 1891 an important pioneering study by Frank Wilson Blackmar (b.1854) was published at Baltimore as a volume in the historical and political science studies of Johns Hopkins University. It bore the title *Spanish institutions in the southwest.* Also in 1891 there appeared at Mexico City the first of two essays under the general title *Época colonial* by Luis Gonzales Obregón (1865-1938). The second volume was published in 1895 at the same place. A corrected and enlarged edition of these was published in one volume at Mexico City in 1900.

A brief but valuable work of 110 pages appeared at Mexico City in 1893 under the title *El arte en México en la época antigua y durante el gobierno virreinal.* The author was Manual Gustavo Antonio Revilla (b.1863). A second edition was published at Mexico City in 1923.

The most extensive work on Mexican history in this century is that by Niceto de Zamacois (d.1886) entitled *Historia de Méjico desde sus tiempos más remotos hasta nuestros días.* Its twenty-two volumes were published in twenty-three at Mexico City between the years 1876 and 1902 and were based upon considerable research.

The largest work in English dealing with Mexico published in this century is *The history of Mexico* (Volumes IX-XIV of his *Works*) by Hubert Howe Bancroft (1832-1918). This appeared at San Francisco between 1883 and 1888 in six volumes. His *History of the north Mexican states and Texas* (Volumes XV and XVI of his *Works*) was published at the same place in two volumes between 1886 and 1889, while his *History of California* (Volumes XVIII-XXIV of his *Works*) was published in seven volumes at San Francisco from 1884 to 1890.

One of the most valuable of nineteenth-century works concerning Mexico is that edited by Vicente Riva Palacio (1832-1896) under the title *México a través de los siglos.* It was published at Mexico City in five volumes between 1887 and 1889. In this treatise all phases of Mexican history and civilization are covered from the earliest times to the date of publication.

3. *Central America (Guatemala)*

Histories of Central America, frequently referred to as "Guatemala" in colonial days and occasionally in the early nineteenth century, are very numerous. In English, Hubert Howe Bancroft's *History of Central America* was for a long time considered a standard treatise. It was published in three volumes at San Francisco between 1882 and 1887, being Volumes VI-VIII of his *Works*.

In Spanish one of the best and most comprehensive works is the seven-volume *Reseña histórica de Centro-America* written by Lorenzo Montúfar y Rivera Maestre (1823-1898). It was published at Guatemala City between 1878 and 1888.

An earlier work is that by Francisco de Paula García Peláez (1785-1867) entitled *Memorias para la historia del antiguo reyno de Guatemala* published in three volumes at Guatemala City in 1851 and 1852. This history treats the region to the year 1821.

A work planned to cover about the same period (from 1502 to 1821) is the *Historia de la América Central* written by José Milla y Vidaurre (1827-1882), the first volume of which appeared at Guatemala City in 1879, while the second volume appeared at the same place in 1882, the year of the author's death. This volume reached only as far as the year 1686. The work was completed in two more volumes by Agustín Gómez Carrillo (b.1842) and was printed in 1895-97, the place unknown. In 1937 at Guatemala City the two volumes by Milla were reprinted under the pseudonym Salomé Gil.

Another general work, with emphasis on native remains, is by John Lloyd Stephens (1805-1852), entitled *Incidents of travel in Central America, Chiapas and Yucatan,* and published originally at London in 1841 in two volumes. Many subsequent editions have appeared, including a one-volume edition, with additions, published first at London in 1854 and at New York the next year. This study is much more than a travel account.

A work dealing with a portion of Central America in the colonial period and one which contains the text of many historical documents from the Archives of the Indies is entitled *Costa Rica, Nicaragua y Panamá en el siglo XVI*. It was edited by Manuel María de Peralta (b.1844) and was published at Madrid in 1883.

One of the earliest works of this century dealing with Central America is entitled *Compendio de la historia de la ciudad de Guatemala,* which, however, covers more of the history of Central America than is indicated by the title. It was written by Domingo Juarros (1752-1820) and was published at Guatemala City in two volumes between 1808 and 1818. An abridged English translation appeared at London in 1823 under the title *A statistical and commercial history of the Kingdom of Guatemala.* A third edition of this work in two volumes was published at Guatemala City in 1937.

A more recent work in Spanish is the *Compendio de historia de la América Central* by Agustín Gómez Carrillo which was published at Madrid in 1892.

Two Spanish works dealing with the independence period in Central America should be mentioned. The first is the *Memorias para la historia de la revolución de Centro-América* by Manuel Montúfar (b.1859), which was published at Jalapa in 1832; and the second is the *Bosquejo historico de las revoluciones de Centro-América* by Alejandro Marure (1809-1851), published at Guatemala City in two volumes in 1837. This latter work deals specifically with the critical period from 1811 to 1834 and was reprinted at Paris and Mexico City in two volumes in 1913.

An English work of some merit which deals with the years 1827 and 1828 is entitled *Guatemala or the republic of Central America.* It was written by Henry Dunn and was published at New York in 1828.

4. *Honduras*

A work in two volumes dealing with Honduras was published at Tegucigalpa in 1882 and 1883 under the title *Compendio de la historia social y política de Honduras.* The work was by Antonio R. Vallejo and was intended as a text for colleges and secondary schools.

An earlier work, by Ephraim George Squier and entitled briefly *Honduras,* was published at London in 1870. This volume is in reality a revised edition of the author's *States of Central America* (New York, 1858) which in turn had been based upon his *Notes on Central America* (New York, 1855).

5. *Nicaragua*

The largest single work on Nicaragua published in this century is the *Historia de Nicaragua desde los tiempos más remotos hasta el año de 1852.* It was written by Tomás Ayón (1821-1887) and was published at Granada in three volumes, 1882-89.

At Managua in Nicaragua in 1889 appeared the *Historia de Nicaragua* by José Dolores Gámez (b.1851). This is a comprehensive treatment of the story of the country from the earliest period to 1860 and gives at the same time the country's relations with Mexico, Central America, and Spain. The Walker episode has been treated by various authors but William Walker's (1824-1860) own account, *The war in Nicaragua* (New York and Mobile, 1860), is the basic one. Another English volume covering a wide variety of subjects but ineffectually written is entitled *Nicaragua.* The author was Peter F. Stout and the book appeared at Philadelphia in 1859. A much better English work is *Nicaragua, . . .* by Ephraim George Squier, published at New York in 1852.

6. *Costa Rica*

In Costa Rica Francisco Montero Barrantes (b.1864) brought out in two volumes at San José (1892-94) his *Elementos de historia de Costa Rica* dealing with the period from 1502 to 1890. A volume by León Fernández (1840-1887) treating the history of Costa Rica from 1502 to 1821 is entitled

Historia de Costa Rica (Madrid, 1889). This book was written while the author was compiling his *Colección de documentos para la historia de Costa Rica* (10 vols., San José, 1881-1907).

7. *West Indies*

Among the general works dealing with the West Indies in this century the following should be mentioned. In 1808 the three-volume *History of the West Indies* by Thomas Coke (1747-1814) was published at Liverpool and dealt largely with missionaries and Methodist missions in each of the islands. In 1827 Thomas Southey's *Chronological history of the West Indies* was published at London in three volumes. Ten years later (1837) at London appeared *The West Indies* by Sir Andrew Halliday (1781-1839), which is of greater value than its size would indicate. In 1847 Adrien Dessales published at Paris his five-volume *Histoire générale des Antilles.* In 1880 a volume entitled *The West Indies* by Charles H. Eden (1839-1900) was published at London.

8. *Cuba*

Several works dealing with Cuba should be mentioned. In 1813 Antonio José Valdés (1780-1836) brought out (the place unknown) his *Historia de la isla de Cuba y en especial de la Habana* which was reprinted in Volume III of *Los tres primeros historiadores de la isla de Cuba* (3 vols., Havana, 1876-77) edited by Rafael Ángel Cowley (1837-1908) and D. Andrés Pego.

In 1826 at Paris appeared as a separate publication the two-volume *Essai politique sur l'île de Cuba* by Alexander von Humboldt. An English edition, with omissions, was published at New York and London in 1856. In 1838 there appeared also at Paris an elaborate work entitled *Histoire physique, politique et naturelle de l'île de Cuba* in two volumes and an atlas. The work, although co-operative, was largely the production of Ramón de la Sagra (1798-1871).

In 1842 Jacobo de la Pezuela y Lobo (1811-1882) published at New York City his *Ensayo histórico de la isla de Cuba* which was followed between 1863 and 1866 at Madrid by his *Diccionario geográfico, estadístico, histórico de la isla de Cuba* and between 1868 and 1878 by his four-volume *Historia de la isla de Cuba,* published at Madrid and New York simultaneously.

During 1865 and 1866 at New York appeared in two volumes the *Historia de la isla de Cuba* by Pedro José Guiteras (1814-1890). A second edition was printed at Havana in three volumes in 1927 and 1928.

In 1872 and 1873 Justo Zaragoza (1833-1896) brought out at Madrid his two-volume work on nineteenth-century disturbances in Cuba entitled *Las insurrecciones en Cuba.* This writer also edited a number of important works.

In 1876 and 1887 the first two volumes of the *Naturaleza y civilización de la grandiosa isla de Cuba* were published at Madrid which covered the story to the year 1602. The author, Miguel Rodríguez Ferrer (1815-1889), left two further volumes unfinished when he died.

From 1895 to 1898 Antonio Pirala y Criado (1824-1903) published at Madrid his three-volume *Anales de la guerra de Cuba* which dealt with the Ten Years' War (1868-78). In 1896 at Chicago Murat Halsted (1829-1908) brought out his *Story of Cuba* which was concerned mainly with the struggle for liberty against Spain, and in 1899 James Morton Callahan (b.1864) published at Baltimore his carefully written *Cuba and international relations.*

9. *Santo Domingo and Haiti*

Because of local disturbed conditions in the island of Santo Domingo or Haiti, many writers turned their attention to this region. In 1801 Bryan Edwards and Sir William Young (1749-1815) published *An historical survey of Saint Domingo* at London. Four years later appeared at the same place *An historical account of the black empire of Hayti* by Marcus Rainsford. This work dealt with Haiti under France to the year 1804.

In 1818 at London Sir James Basket brought out his *History of the Island of St. Domingo from its first discovery by Columbus.* This was followed by a reprint in New York in 1824.

In 1826 at Paris appeared the *Histoire politique et statistique de l'île d'Hayti* by a person using the pseudonym Placido Justin (b.1777). The same year and the following was published in three volumes at Dresden the *Geschichte des freistaats von St. Domingo* by Karl Ferdinand Philippi. In 1837 Jonathan Brown published in two volumes at Philadelphia his delightful *History and present condition of St. Domingo.*

In 1846 at Paris was printed in two volumes Romuald Le Pelletier de Saint-Remy's (1809-1882) *Saint Dominique, étude et solution nouvelle de la question haitienne.* In the following two years (1847 and 1848) there appeared at Port-au-Prince Thomas Madiou's *Histoire d'Haiti* in three volumes, dealing with the story of the island from 1492 to 1807. A second edition of this work was published at Port-au-Prince in three volumes in 1922 and 1923. In 1853 at Havana appeared the first volume (600 pages) of the *Historia de Santo Domingo desde su descubrimiento hasta nuestros días* by Antonio del Monte y Tejada.

Between 1853 and 1858 appeared at Paris the eight-volume illustrated *Étude sur l'histoire d'Haiti* by B. Ardouin (1796-1865).

In 1867 or 1869 at Santo Domingo City appeared José Gabriel García's (1834-1910) *Compendio de la historia de Santo Domingo,* which carried the story of the island to 1865. A second edition (Santo Domingo City, 1879) continued the history to 1876. Finally, between 1893 and 1900, the complete work in three volumes was published at Santo Domingo City.

In 1873 Samuel Hazard's (1834-1876) *Santo Domingo past and present, with a glance at Hayti,* was published simultaneously at New York and London. In 1884 a popular volume entitled *Hayti or the black republic* was published at London, the author being Sir Spencer Buckingham St. John (1825-1910). Two years later the book was translated into French and published at Paris. In 1884 also appeared at Madrid a detailed two-volume study entitled *Anexión y guerra de Santo Domingo* by José de la Gándara y Navarro (1820-1885). Two years later Jacques Nicholas Léger (b.1859), one of the foremost Haitian writers, published at Paris his *La politique extérieure d'Haiti.* In 1899 there appeared at Paris the *Histoire militaire de la révolution de Saint Dominque* by Isidore Henry de Poyen-Bellisle (b.1839).

10. Puerto Rico

A comprehensive work dealing with Puerto Rico was published at London in 1834 under the title, briefly cited, *An account of the present state of the island of Puerto Rico.* The author was George Dawson Flinter (d.1839).

11. Colombia

Works dealing with Colombia are both numerous and valuable. In 1822 there was printed at London a two-volume work by Alexander Walker entitled *Colombia, being a geographical, statistical, agricultural, commercial, and political account of that country.* At the same time the work was indifferently translated into Spanish in two volumes and also published at London. Three years later, in 1825, Francis Hall (d.1833) brought out his popular *Colombia: its present state, . . . ,* at London. A second edition appeared two years later.

In 1827 at Paris appeared in ten volumes and an atlas the monumental *Historia de la revolución de la república de Colombia* by José Manuel Restrepo (1781-1863). The next year Ernst Münch published at Dresden in two volumes his *Die geschichte von Colombia.*

In 1848 appeared at Paris Joaquín Acosta's (1799-1852) *Compendio histórico,* which dealt with the discovery and colonization of New Granada in the sixteenth century. A second edition did not appear until 1901 at Bogotá.

In 1869 at Bogotá was published the three-volume *Historia eclesiástica y civil de Nueva Granada* by José Manuel Groot (1800-1878). A second edition in five volumes appeared at Bogotá between 1889 and 1893.

In 1872 at Poissy appeared the two-volume *Historia de la Compañia de Jesús en la Nueva Granada* by José Joaquín Borda (1835-1878).

In 1882 at Barranquilla appeared the first 225 pages of the *Historia de Colombia* by Carlos Benedetti. A second and complete edition was published in 1887 at Lima. In 1883 at Bogotá a work of considerable value to historians by Soledad Acosta de Samper appeared, entitled *Biografías de hombres ilustres o notables de la época del descubrimiento y colonización de Colombia.* During the next two years (1884-85) there appeared in a third edition at Bogotá the three-volume *Leyendas históricas* by Luis Capella Toledo. The date of the first edition is not known.

In 1896 and 1898 appeared at Valladolid the three-volume history of *La Compañía de Jesús en Colombia y Centro-America después de su restauración* written by Rafael Pérez (1842-1901). The next year, in 1899, at Santiago, Chile, José Toribio Medina published his *Historia del tribunal del santo oficio de la inquisición de Cartagena de las indias,* which constitutes a companion volume to his work dealing with the same subject in Peru.

12. *Venezuela*

Of the works dealing with Venezuela the following may be noted. In 1806 at Paris appeared three volumes briefly entitled *Voyage à la partie oriental de la terre-ferme* by François Raymond Joseph de Pons (1751-1812), often incorrectly spelled Deponds. The author spent the years 1801 to 1804 in the territory and gives the history of the country in connection with his observations. An English edition in two volumes appeared at London in 1807, and an excellent Spanish edition was published at Caracas in 1930.

In 1841 the three-volume *Resumen de la historia de Venezuela* of Rafael María Baralt (1810-1860) and Ramón Díaz was published at Paris in two sections, the first in one volume by Baralt alone covering the period to 1797 and the second section in two volumes covering the period from 1797 to 1837. In 1887 at Caracas appeared a new three-volume edition of this work, while at Paris appeared a French edition in 1939.

In 1875 at Paris was printed a volume by Miguel Tejera (b.1848) entitled *Compendio de la historia de Venezuela* covering the subject to about 1870. This was followed by two volumes (Paris, 1875-78) entitled *Venezuela pintoresca e ilustrada* dealing with the same period.

In 1881 at Caracas appeared a valuable discussion of heroes and campaigns of the War for Independence entitled *Venezuela heróica* by Eduardo Blanco (1838-1912). In 1935 at Caracas appeared the eleventh edition of this work.

During 1890 and 1891 Arístides Rojas (1826-1894) brought out at Caracas his *Historia patria. Leyendas históricas de Venezuela* in two volumes. In 1891 appeared at the same place his *Estudios históricos* dealing with the origins of the country. Finally, in 1919 at Madrid, appeared his *Capítulos de la historia colonial de Venezuela.* In 1893 appeared at Barcelona the first volume of the *Historia contemporánea de Venezuela* by L. Level de Goda covering political and military affairs from 1858 to 1886.

One of the best works on military history in the early national period is the *Bosquejo de la historia militar de Venezuela en la guerra de su independencia,* the first volume of which was published at Valencia in 1857.

13. *Ecuador*

In Ecuador Pedro Fermín Ceballos (b.1814) brought out in five volumes his *Resumen de la historia del Ecuador* in 1870. The work was published in Lima and covered the history of the country from the earliest times to 1845. The author, the chief Ecuadorian historian of the nineteenth century, intended to issue a sixth volume, but because of errors it was suspended and did not appear until 1888 at Lima, and then with the title *Geografía de la república del Ecuador.*

In 1881 at Quito appeared the brief *Historia eclesiástica del Ecuador* by Archbishop Federico González Suárez (1844-1917), covering the period from 1520 to 1600. In 1890 the same author began to bring out his excellent *Historia general de la república del Ecuador.* This work was completed in nine volumes, including an atlas, in 1903 and was printed at Quito. However, it only covers the colonial period.

In 1885 at Quito appeared the first edition of *El Ecuador 1825-1875* by Pedro Moncayo (1804-1888) and in 1892 Augustine Berthe (1830-1907) published his partisan *García Moreno presidente de la república del Ecuador* in two volumes at Paris.

An English work dealing with Ecuador was written by the mountain climber and teacher, Edward Whymper (1840-1911). It is entitled *Travels among the great Andes of the equator.* It was published with a "Supplementary Appendix" in two volumes at London, 1891-92. A one-volume edition appeared at New York in 1892. The book is more than a descriptive treatise.

14. *Peru*

Among the writings in this century on Peru is the classic *History of the conquest of Peru* by William Hickling Prescott, published in two volumes at New York and Paris in 1847 and in many other editions subsequently.

In 1858 José de la Riva Agüero (1783-1858), under the pseudonym of P. Pruvonena, published his important explanatory *Memorias y documentos para la historia de la independencia del Perú* in two volumes at Paris.

A work of great value to historians, although it is not a history in the strict sense, is the ten-volume *Documentos históricos del Perú en las épocas del coloniaje después de la conquista y de la independencia hasta la presente.* The work appeared at Lima, 1863-77, and was edited and compiled by Manuel de Odriozola.

At Lima in 1863 Ricardo Palma (1833-1919) brought out his classic volume entitled *Anales de la inquisición de Lima.* Among his other productions should be mentioned his *Perú. Tradiciones,* first published at Lima in two volumes in 1875-77 and followed by a second edition in six volumes in 1883. A new edition at Madrid reached six volumes in 1923.

Between 1868 and 1874 at Lima appeared the three-volume *Historia del Perú independiente, 1822-1827,* by Marino Felipe Paz Soldán (1821-1886). This work was reprinted at Lima in two volumes in 1919. In 1929 a new three-volume edition was published at the same place with additions to the year 1833.

A work dealing with religious affairs is the *Apuntes para la historia eclesiástica del Perú hasta el gobierno del VII arzobispo* by Manuel Tovar (1844-1907), which was published in two volumes at Lima 1873 and 1876. Meanwhile, in 1874 at the same place was published the brief secondary textbook entitled *Historia del Perú,* written by Agustín de la Rosa Toro. In the same year at Lima appeared the first volume of the indispensable *Diccionario histórico-biográfico del Perú* by Manuel de Mendiburu (1805-1886). This was completed in eight volumes, the last being published at Lima in 1890. In 1931 the first volume of a new edition of the work appeared at Madrid, likewise to be completed in eight volumes. In 1874 also appeared at Lima the first of six volumes (1874-1911) entitled *El Perú,* which constituted a historical geography of that country. The author was Antonio Raimondi (1826-1890), a widely known Peruvian geologist.

In 1879 and 1880 at Caracas appeared the nine-volume *Memorias* of General Florencio O'Leary (b.1801), Volumes XXVII and XXVIII of which bear the title *Bolívar y la emancipación de Sur-América.* These volumes were republished at Madrid in 1915. The first volume covers the period from 1783 to 1819, while the second treats the years 1819 to 1826.

In 1886 Ricardo Cappa published at Lima his secondary text entitled *Historia compendiada del Perú* in two volumes. The next year at Santiago José Toribio Medina brought out his scholarly two-volume *Historia del tribunal del santo oficio de la inquisición de Lima,* which deals with the subject between the years 1569 and 1820.

In 1894 at Lima appeared the brief but valuable *Estado social del Perú durante la dominación española* written by Javier Prado y Ugarteche (b.1871). Three years later at Madrid was published the brilliant two-volume *Bolívar en el Perú* by Gonzalo Bulnes (1851-1936), which dealt with the Liberator's last campaigns in that country. This work had been preceded by his two-volume *Historia de la expedición libertadora del Perú* (Santiago, 1887-88), covering the years 1817 to 1822. In 1899 appeared at Lima the *Resumen de historia del Perú* by Carlos Wiesse (b.1859), which has come to be considered the best general secondary textbook published in Peru.

The best general work in English on Peruvian history is by Sir Clements Markham entitled *A history of Peru,* published at Chicago in 1892.

One of the leading historians of Peru in this century was Sebastián Lorente (d.1884). Among his writings are the *Historia antigua del Perú* (Lima, 1860), the *Historia de la conquista del Perú* (Lima, 1861), the *Historia del Perú bajo la dinastía austriaca, 1542-1598* (Lima, 1863), the *Historia del Perú* (Lima, 1866), and the *Historia del Perú bajo los Borbones, 1700-1821* (Lima, 1871).

15. Bolivia

Among works dealing with Bolivia and written in this century three may be noted. In 1874 at Santiago, Chile, appeared the valuable *Estudio histórico de Bolivia* which dealt especially with the administration of José María de Achá but in reality covered the period from 1825 to 1868. The author was the Chilean historian Ramón Sotomayor y Valdés (b.1830). In 1896 appeared the *Compendio de historia de Bolivia* by José María Carnacho, and in this and the two following years Gabriel René Moreno (1834-1908) published at Santiago, Chile, his *Ultimos días coloniales en el Alto-Perú* (two volumes in one). A new two-volume edition of this work was printed at La Paz in 1940.

16. Paraguay

Of the works about Paraguay in this century one of the earliest is that published at Paris in 1809 in four volumes and an atlas under the title *Voyages dans l'Amérique meridional* (from 1781 to 1801), by Félix de Azara (1746-1821). This work, which dealt chiefly with the natural history of the whole La Plata region, had been enlarged by other writers from the previous editions of 1801 (2 vols., Paris), 1802 (2 vols., Madrid), and 1805 (3 vols., Madrid). In 1896 at Asunción the work was printed in two volumes under the title *Descripción é historia del Paraguay y del Río de la Plata.*

In 1827 at Paris appeared another French work of some importance by Johann Rudolph Rengger (1795-1832) and R. de Longchamp under the title *Essai historique sur la révolution du Paraguay.* The volume deals at considerable length with the dictator Francia. An English edition appeared at London the same year as the French. Another work by a Frenchman was entitled *La république du Paraguay* (Brussels, 1862). The author was a nobleman named Alfred Louis Hubert Chislain Marbais du Graty (1823-1891). Still another French volume appeared at Marseilles in 1867 under the title *Le Paraguay moderne* and dealt with the history and geography of the country, besides containing considerable statistic information. The author was Benjamin Poncel (1807-1872). A fifth French work is entitled *Le Paraguay.* It was written by A. P. F. Lambel (1814-ca. 1900), and it appeared at Tours in 1878. A sixth work written by a Frenchman, who became a Brazilian citizen, bore the title *Historia da republica jesuitica do Paraguay.* The author was João Pedro Gay (b.1815), and his study appeared in book form in 1881 at Rio de Janeiro, after being published serially. A seventh work originally written in French by E. de Bourgade La Dardye (b.1854) is entitled *Le Paraguay.* It was published at Paris in 1889. In 1892 it was translated into English and published at London under the title *Paraguay, the land, and the people, . . .*

An important work in Spanish which bears the title *Historia de los gobernantes del Paraguay* was published at Buenos Aires in 1887. The author was Antonio Zinny (1821-1890), and his volume deals with the history of the country from 1535 to 1887.

Two works in English of value for the historian were printed in this century. The first is entitled *Letters on Paraguay,* written by John Parish Robertson (1792-1843) and W. P. Robertson and published in three volumes at London in 1839. Volume III is devoted to Francia and is entitled *Francia's reign of terror.* The second is a briefer work in two volumes written by Charles A. Washburn (1822-1889) and published at Boston in 1871 under the title *The history of Paraguay.* Based upon personal observations and reminiscences of the author's diplomatic activities, it is somewhat biased.

17. *Argentina*

Argentine history was the subject of numerous treatises in the nineteenth century. One of the earliest was published in three volumes at Buenos Aires in 1816 under the title *Ensayo de la historia civil del Paraguay, Buenos Aires y Tucumán.* The author was Gregorio Funes (1749-1830). A second edition of this work appeared at Buenos Aires in two volumes in 1856.

A still earlier work, but considerably shorter, is that by Samuel Hull Wilcocke entitled the *History of the viceroyalty of Buenos Aires* (London, 1807), which was written while the English held the city. The subject matter covered is varied and comprehensive, and the author considers the region a British colony.

In 1825 at London appeared Spanish and English editions of Ignacio Benito Núñez's (1792-1846) *Noticias históricas,* dealing with the United Provinces of the Río de la Plata. This work was published in the form of a letter of 323 pages which aimed to inform the British ministry of the Brazilian usurpation of Uruguay.

In 1836 a work of great value to historians began to appear at Buenos Aires. It was entitled *Colección de obras y documentos relativos a la historia antigua y moderna de las provincias del Río de la Plata* (6 vols., Buenos Aires, 1836-37). The author was Pedro de Angelis (1784-1859), a noted compiler and editor. A new edition of the work was printed in the same place in five volumes in 1910.

In 1839 appeared at London the first edition of Sir Woodbine Parish's (1792-1882) *Buenos Ayres and the provinces of the Río de la Plata.* Since the author was an explorer, his account contains much geographical and anthropological information.

In the same year (1839), appeared the valuable *Narrative of the surveying voyages of His Majesty's ships Adventure and Beagle, between the years 1826 and 1836,* . . . by Philip Parker King (1793-1856), Robert Fitzroy (1805-1865), and Charles Darwin (1809-1882). The work, first published at London in four volumes, contains important facts concerning southern Argentina which are of considerable value to historians.

In 1845 at Santiago, Chile, was published *Civilización i barbarie* by the great Argentine statesman and writer, Domingo Faustino Sarmiento (1811-1888). This work has been issued in many editions, the first French edition appearing at Paris in 1853. The second Spanish edition was printed at Santiago in 1851. A third Spanish edition, which seems to be a reprint of the second, date and place not known, was translated into English by Mrs. Horace Mann and printed at New York in 1868 under the title *Life in the Argentine Republic in the days of the tyrants, or civilization and barbarism.* At the same time the work was issued at London. Sarmiento is known as a writer in many fields including history, biography, literature, criticism, politics, economics, sociology, religion, and education, dealing chiefly with Argentina and Chile. His *Obras* appeared first in Spanish (52 vols., Santiago, Chile, 1887-1902) and an index volume (Buenos Aires, 1903). A French edition of his *Works* appeared at Paris (53 vols., 1889-1909).

In 1850 at Paris was published the *Considérations historiques et politiques sur les républiques de la Plata* by Alfred de Brossard. Eight years later (1858) there appeared at Paris *La Confédération argentine* by the French Baron Alfred Louis Hubert Chislain Marbais du Graty.

In 1861 at Buenos Aires appeared the *Historia argentina* by Luis L. Domínguez (b.1810), which covered the period from 1492 to 1820. Two years later, in 1863, appeared at Buenos Aires in two volumes the *Lecciones sobre la historia de la república argentina* by José Manuel Estrada (1842-1894). A second edition was published at Buenos Aires in 1898.

A general descriptive work of value to the historian is the *Description géographique et statistique de la confédération argentine* (Paris, 1860-73), published in three volumes and an atlas. The author was the Frenchman Jean Antoine Victor Martin de Moussy (1810-1869).

In 1877 and 1878 there appeared at Montevideo, twelve volumes in six, the valuable *Historia política y militar de las repúblicas del Plata* by Antonio Díaz which covers the period from 1828 to 1866.

Between 1879 and 1882 the *Historia de los gobernadores de las provincias argentinas* by Antonio Zinny was printed at Buenos Aires in three volumes. This covered the period from 1810 to 1881. In 1920 and 1921 the work was reissued in a revised edition of five volumes at Buenos Aires. The same author published at Buenos Aires in 1875 his valuable *Bibliografía histórica de las provincias unidas del Río de la Plata,* which covered the period from 1780 to 1821.

From 1883 to 1893 at Buenos Aires appeared the *Historia de la república argentina* in ten volumes by Vicente Fidel López (1815-1903). Because of the author's death the work was never completed and the story ended with the year 1829. In 1896 the same author's *Manual de la historia argentina* was published at Buenos Aires.

In 1887 appeared in a definitive edition (3 vols., Buenos Aires) Bartolomé Mitre's *Historia de Belgrano y de la independencia argentina.* In the two following years (1888 and 1889) the three-volume *Historia argentina* of Mariano A. Pelliza (1837-1902) was published at Buenos Aires. In 1894 his *La dictadura de Rosas* appeared at Buenos Aires, and was followed in 1897 at the same place by his *Historia de la organización nacional.* Parts of the foregoing works had appeared in the author's *Historia argentina.*

In 1892 appeared at Buenos Aires the five-volume *Historia de la confederación argentina* by Adolfo Saldías (1859-1914). This is the second edition which had been revised and corrected and covers about the years 1817 to 1870. An entirely new edition of the work was published in nine volumes at Buenos Aires in 1929 and 1930. The original edition of the work had appeared at Paris in three volumes between 1881 and 1887 under the title *Historia de Rosas y su época.*

A work of great historical value was published in two volumes at Buenos Aires in 1893 under the title *Historia de los medios de comunicación y transporte en la república argentina.* The author was Ramón J. Cárcano (b.1860).

In 1899 at Buenos Aires Martín García Mérou (1862-1905) published his *Historia de la república argentina* in two volumes, the first of which carries the story to 1800. Shortly before this volume appeared Francisco Ramos Mejía (1847-1893) wrote his *Historia de la evolución argentina* which, however, was not published until after his death, when the first volume appeared at Buenos Aires in 1921.

18. *Uruguay*

Of the histories of Uruguay several should be mentioned. In 1864 at Paris were published two volumes of the *Apuntes para la historia de la república oriental del Uruguay desde el año de 1810 hasta el del 1852* by Antonio Deodoro de Pascal. The work seems never to have been completed and the story was carried only to the year 1829.

In 1879 and 1880 appeared a work of considerable aid to historians with the title *Rasgos biográficos de hombres notables de la república oriental del*

Uruguay. It was written by Isidoro De-Marie (1815-1906) and was published in three volumes at Montevideo. In 1939 at Montevideo the work was reissued in four volumes in a revised edition. The first edition of this valuable compilation had been preceded by the same author's great work entitled *Compendio de la historia de la república oriental del Uruguay,* the place and date of the first edition unknown. Volume I appeared in a second edition at Montevideo in 1867, while the whole work, six volumes in three, was published at Montevideo in 1895 in a seventh edition.

In 1881 at the same place was published the *Bosquejo histórico de la república oriental del Uruguay* in its third revised edition, the first printing being at Montevideo in 1866. This covers the history of the region from the discovery to 1830. The author was Francisco A. Berra (b.1844).

In 1886 Eliza J. M. Clemens published at Philadelphia *La Plata countries of South America.* Two years later at Montevideo appeared a volume entitled *Apuntes sobre la historia de la república oriental del Uruguay* by Julián O. Nuranda (b.1854). Between 1912 and 1916 the work was published in two volumes as a textbook. In 1898 the same author brought out at Montevideo his one-volume *Compendio de historia del Uruguay* which dealt with the period between 1830 and 1898.

In 1892 at Montevideo was published Victor Arreguine's (1865-1924) *Historia del Uruguay.* Eight years later, in 1900, the short *Historia de la república oriental del Uruguay* by Pablo Blanco Acevedo was published at Montevideo.

Among the most important works dealing with this region is the three-volume *Historia de la dominación española en Uruguay* written by Francisco Bauzá (1851-1899) and published at Montevideo from 1880 to 1882. The first edition carries the story to the year 1817. A second edition of three volumes was published at Montevideo between 1895 and 1897 and continues the story to 1830. In 1929 a third edition was published at the same place.

19. *Chile*

Chile produced some of the most prolific historical writers of the nineteenth century. Among these are Benjamín Vicuña Mackenna (1831-1886), José Toribio Medina (1852-1930), Miguel Luis Amunátegui (1828-1888), and Diego Barros Arana (1830-1907).

Among the nineteenth-century works of Vicuña Mackenna should be mentioned his *Historia jeneral de la república de Chile* (5 vols., Santiago, 1866-83, written in collaboration with others), *Historia de los diez años de la administración de Don Manuel Montt* (5 vols., Santiago, 1860-63), *Guerra del Pacífico* (2 vols., Santiago, 1880), *Chile: relaciones históricas* (2 vols., Santiago, 1877-78), *La guerra á muerte* (Santiago, 1868), *Chile: episodios marítimos* (Santiago, 1879), *Historia de la guerra de Chile con*

España (Santiago, 1883), *Los orígenes de las familias chilenas* (Santiago, 1903), and numerous biographies, and so on.

The chief historical writings of Medina in this century are his *Los aborígenes de Chile* (Santiago, 1882), *Cosas de la colonia* (2 vols., Santiago, 1889 and 1910), *Historia del tribunal del santo oficio de la inquisición en Chile* (2 vols., Santiago, 1890, which amplifies his similar work on the Inquisition in Lima, published at Lima in two volumes in 1887), *Descubrimiento del Río de las Amazonas* (Sevilla, 1894, which was translated by Bertram T. Lee [d. 1937] and published in English by the American Geographical Society at New York in 1934), *Juan Díaz de Solís* (2 vols., Santiago, 1897), and *Historia de la literatura colonial de Chile* (3 vols., Santiago, 1878).

In this century Amunátegui published his one-volume *Compendio de la historia política y eclesiástica de Chile* (Valparaiso, 1856), *La crónica de 1810* (3 vols., Santiago, 1876-99), *Los precursores de la independencia de Chile* (3 vols., Santiago, 1870-72), *La dictadura de O'Higgins* (Santiago, 1853), *Descubrimiento i conquista de Chile* (Santiago, 1862), *La reconquista española de Chile en 1814* (Santiago, 1851), *Ensayos biográficos* (4 vols., Santiago, 1893-96), and so on.

The largest single historical work on Chile in the nineteenth century is that in sixteen volumes by Diego Barros Arana entitled *Historia jeneral de Chile* (Santiago, 1884-1902). This began to appear in a second revised edition at Santiago in 1930. This immensely valuable work was made more useful by the publication of an index volume listing 7,037 names. It was prepared by Carlos Vicuña Mackenna and entitled *Indice de la Historia general de Chile de don Diego Barros Arana* (Santiago, 1936). Barros Arana's *Historia jeneral de la independencia de Chile* (4 vols., Santiago, 1854-58) is also of great value.

A number of other important works of considerable value should be mentioned. In 1850 appeared at Valparaiso the three-volume *Historia eclesiástica, política y literaria de Chile* by José Ignacio Victor Eyzaguirre. A French edition of this work was published in three volumes at Lille in 1855.

During 1877 and 1878 there appeared at Valparaiso the three-volume *Historia general de el reyno de Chile* (to 1810) by Diego de Rosales. In 1889 at Santiago was published the first edition of Pedro Pablo Figueroa's (1857-1909) *Historia de la revolución constituyente,* which was written from the documents and covered the years 1858 and 1859.

Toward the end of the century Ramón Pacheco (1845-1888) prepared his monumental *Episodios de la guerra del Pacifico* in 20 volumes. This work, however, was not printed until the years 1936 to 1940.

In 1891 at Barcelona was printed the two-volume *Historia de la Compañía de Jesús en Chile* by Francisco Enrich (1817-1883). An earlier and even more important and extensive work upon religious activities in Chile, as well as other parts of South America, is the *Storia della missioni apostoliche dello stato del Chile,* published in four volumes at Rome in 1827. The author was Giuseppe Sallusti.

In 1893 a work on Chile appeared in English with the title *A history of Chile.* The book, printed at Chicago, was written by Anson Uriel Hancock.

In 1899 at Valparaiso Daniel Riquelme brought out his *Compendio de historia de Chile.* The next year was published the two-volume *Historia natural, militar, civil y sagarda del reino de Chile* at Santiago by José Pérez García (1726-1814), which carried the account from the earliest times to about 1800. The work had been written almost a century before it appeared in print.

Between 1900 and 1903 appeared the four-volume *Historia de Chile bajo el gobierno del jeneral D. Joaquín Prieto* by Ramón Sotomayor y Valdés. The first two volumes were published in this edition for the second time in a revised and corrected form.

CHAPTER FIVE

TWENTIETH CENTURY WORKS

A. Introduction
B. General works
   1. In English
   2. In foreign languages
C. Works on individual countries and regions
   1. Brazil
   2. Mexico
   3. Spanish Florida
   4. Central America (Guatemala)
   5. Honduras
   6. Nicaragua
   7. Costa Rica
   8. El Salvador
   9. Panama
   10. West Indies (Cuba)
   11. Dominican Republic
   12. Haiti
   13. Puerto Rico
   14. Colombia
   15. Venezuela
   16. Ecuador
   17. Peru
   18. Bolivia
   19. Paraguay
   20. Argentina
   21. Uruguay
   22. Chile

A. Introduction

In the twentieth century, and particularly after the first decade, an increased interest was centered in Hispanic America by the nations of the world and especially by the people of the United States. At the same time an earnest attempt was made to understand and to interpret the history and civilization of these peoples both in popular works, such as travel accounts, and in scholarly histories and school textbooks. The people of Hispanic America themselves became aware of their growing importance in world affairs and in a comparatively short time have produced many valuable historical treatises.

B. General Works

1. In English

Among the general treatises written in this century in English are many volumes which can be, or have been, used as textbooks for students in the

United States. The following may be cited as of some importance. In 1901 at New York were published Henry William Brown's (1858-1906) *Latin America* which concerned religious affairs; the *South American republics*, a geographical reader, by W. F. Marwick (1848-1911) and W. A. Smith (b.1866); and Julian Hawthorne's (b.1846) *Spanish America*. In 1903-04 at New York appeared in two volumes the very helpful *South American republics* by Thomas C. Dawson (b.1865). In the latter year at London the journalist Charles Edmond Akers (1861-1915) brought out his important volume entitled *A history of South America from 1854*, which was added to by Lilian Elwyn Elliott and published under the same title at New York in 1930. A most important work published in the same year (1904) is *Spain in America, 1450-1580*, by Edward Gaylord Bourne.

In 1907 at New York C. R. Enock (b.1868) published *The Andes and the Amazon*. This was followed at London in 1909 by *The great Pacific coast* which gave an account of the states of America bordering on the Pacific; *The secret of the Pacific* (New York, 1912), which gave an account of the early civilizations of the area; *The Republics of Central and South America* (New York, 1913); and *Spanish America* (2 vols., London, 1920).

In 1912 W. H. Koebel (1872-1923) published at London his *South America*, followed by *The South Americans* (London, 1915) and his *South America. An industrial and commercial field* (London and New York, 1918). In 1913 at Cleveland the somewhat fantastic yet thought-provoking *History of South America* by W. F. Griewe (b.1852) was published. The year following, the valuable essay by W. R. Shepherd (1871-1934), entitled *Latin America*, was printed at New York, and in 1921 his equally valuable and popularly written volume entitled *The Hispanic nations of the New World* was published at New York.

In 1919 the first true college textbook appeared at New York under the title *A History of Latin America* (revised in 1929). The author was W. W. Sweet (b.1881). This text was followed by a second in 1922 when W. S. Robertson (b.1873) published at New York the first edition of his *History of the Latin American nations* as a text for colleges. The most recent edition, with some added material, appeared in 1932. In 1923 at New York appeared a college text entitled *The republics of Latin America* by H. G. James (b.1887) and P. A. Martin (1879-1942). The next strictly college text did not appear until 1930, when Mary W. Williams (b.1878) published at New York her volume entitled *Peoples and politics of Latin America* (revised in 1938). The next text appeared in 1931 in a preliminary edition entitled *A history of Hispanic America* by A. Curtis Wilgus (b.1897). This, unlike the previous volumes, was intended as a textbook handbook for college students. Another text is that by J. Fred Rippy (b.1892) published at New York in 1932 under the title *Historical evolution of Hispanic America*. A supplement to these textbooks is *Readings in Hispanic American history* by N. Andrew N. Cleven (b.1874), published at Boston in 1927. Still other recent textbooks in English are *A History of Latin America* by David R. Moore (published at New York in 1938); *Latin America, a brief history* by F. A. Kirkpatrick (b.1861), published at New York in 1939; *An outline history of Latin America* by A. Curtis Wilgus and Raul d'Eça (b.1896) published at New York in 1939 with a new edition in 1941; *An introduction to Hispanic American history* by Tom Jones published at New York in 1939; *A short history of the Americas* by R. S. Cotterill published at New York in 1939; and *The development of Hispanic America* by A. Curtis Wilgus published at New York in 1941.

In recent years a number of important works have appeared dealing with Hispanic America in general but at the same time treating special phases of its history and civilization.

In 1901 at London, Robert Gallnigad Bontine Cunninghame Graham (1852-1936) published *A vanished Arcadia* which treated the history of the Jesuits in Paraguay between the years 1607 and 1767. In the following years appeared his *Hernando de Soto* (London, 1903), *Bernal Díaz del Castillo* (New York and London, 1915), *The conquest of New Granada* (London, 1922), *The conquest of the River Plate* (New York, 1924), *Pedro de Valdivia, conqueror of Chile* (New York and London, 1927), and other volumes.

Between 1901 and 1905 appeared in two volumes at New York and London the scholarly and indispensable *Spanish settlements within the present limits of the United States* by Woodbury Lowery (1853-1906).

In 1902 Henry Vignaud (1830-1922) published his critical and careful study on *Toscanelli and Columbus* at London. The next year the work appeared at the same place in a new edition of two volumes in one, which contained many of the author's letters on the subject to Sir Clements Markham and C. Raymond Beasley.

In 1902-03 there appeared at Berlin in English Arthur Baessler's (1857-1907) *Ancient Peruvian art.* The German edition was published the same year at Leipzig.

In 1907 Lewis Spence (b.1874) brought out the first of a series of volumes dealing with early native cultures and civilizations. In that year appeared at London his *Mythologies of Mexico and Peru.* This was followed by *The Popol Vuh* (London, 1908), *Civilizations of ancient Mexico* (New York, 1912), *Myths of the North American Indians* (London, 1914), *The Gods of Mexico* (London, 1922), *The magic and mysteries of Mexico* (London and Philadelphia, 1930), and many other books.

In 1908 Bernard Moses (1846-1930) published at New York his *South America on the eve of emancipation.* This work had been preceded in 1898 by *The establishment of Spanish rule in America.* In 1914 he brought out at New York the two volumes entitled *The Spanish dependencies in South America,* which were followed in 1919 at Berkeley by *Spain's declining power in America,* in 1922 at New York by *Spanish colonial literature in South America,* in 1926 at New York by *The intellectual background of the revolutions in South America,* and in 1929 at New York by his *Spain overseas.* These volumes are extremely useful and are so well done that their author won the reputation as a leading authority in the field.

In 1908 H. C. Lea (1825-1909) published his classic work entitled *The inquisition in the Spanish dependencies* at New York as part of his general history of the Inquisition.

In 1908 also appeared at New York *The other Americans* by Arthur Ruhl (b.1876), and two years later Charles Domville-Fife published at London and New York *The great states of South America* which appeared in a revised edition in 1920 under the title *The states of South America.* In 1922 he published at New York and London *The real South America,* a revised edition of which was published at New York in 1931 under the title *Modern South America.*

In 1910 at London Sir Clements Markham published his useful volume entitled *The Incas of Peru,* which was followed two years later at the same place by his *Conquest of New Granada.* Also in 1910 C. H. Haring (b.1885) brought out at London and New York *The buccaneers in the West Indies in the XVII century.* This was followed by an even more valuable book based upon scholarly research entitled *Trade and navigation between Spain and the Indies in the time of the Hapsburgs* (Cambridge, Mass., 1918).

In 1911 Georges Clemenceau (1841-1929) published at New York his discerning volume entitled *South America today.* The next year at London appeared James Bryce's (1838-1922) valuable work entitled *South America. Observations and impressions.* In the same year at New York was published the first of several careful treatises on American archaeology by Thomas A Joyce (b.1878), entitled *South American archaeology.* In 1914 at London appeared his *Mexican archaeology,* and in 1916 at London was published his *Central American and West Indian archaeology.*

In 1913 Francisco García Calderón (b.1883) published at London and New York his thought-provoking essay entitled *Latin America. Its rise and progress.* In the same year at London appeared A. Henry Savage-Landor's (1865-1924) profusely illustrated two-volume work entitled *Across unknown South America.* In 1914 Rafael Reyes (b.1851) brought out at New York an English translation of his Spanish work entitled *The two Americas.* In 1914, also, a well-written work dealing with the Norse discoveries of America was published at New York. It bore the title *The voyages of the Norsemen to America* and contained eighty-three illustrations and seven maps. The author was George William Hovgaard (b.1857). Two years later Alfred Coester (b.1874) published the first edition of his invaluable *Literary history of Spanish America* at New York. It was translated into Spanish and published at Madrid in 1929.

In 1915 Professor H. E. Bolton (b.1870), one of the leading scholars in the field of Hispanic American history in the United States, published at Berkeley his *Texas in the middle eighteenth century.* This dealt with the Spanish colonial administration in the region. The next year at New York he brought out a volume entitled *Spanish explorations in the southwest, 1542-1706.* In 1921 appeared *The Spanish borderlands* (New Haven), which dealt with the Spaniards in Florida and the Southwest. Many other volumes of a more special character have since come from his facile and scholarly pen.

In 1920 Leo Wiener (1862-1939) brought out the first volume of his *Africa and the discovery of America,* which aimed to show the early influence of African life, customs, and thought upon the American Indians. The work was completed in three volumes at Philadelphia in 1922.

In 1922 at New York and London Clark Wissler (b.1870) published his valuable and indispensable volume on *The American Indian* (printed in a new edition at the same places in 1938).

In 1926 at Berkeley appeared Lilian Fisher's (b.1891) *Viceregal administration in the Spanish American colonies,* and in 1929 appeared at the same place *The intendant system in Spanish America.* A more localized volume by the same author is *The background of the revolution for Mexican independence* (Boston, 1934).

Also in 1926 a specialized treatise in English entitled *The economic geography of South America* by R. H. Whitbeck (1871-1939) was published at New York which treated the geographical and economic aspects of history. A new revised edition was published at New York in 1940. A somewhat similar volume by an Englishman, E. W. Shanahan (b.1882), entitled *South America. An economic and regional geography with an historical chapter,* was published at New York in 1927. The next year Clarence F. Jones (b.1893) published his volume on *The commerce of South America,* which proved of considerable value to historians, and in 1930 be brought out an even more valuable work entitled *South America,* showing the interrelations of history and geography. In 1929 appeared at New York *The new map of South America* by Herbert Adams Gibbons (1880-1934), which stresses more of the historical part of the picture and less of its economic aspects. In 1931 J. F. Normano (b.1890) published at New York his *Struggle for South America,* which gave many historical examples of political and social reaction to the economic exploitation of South America by foreign capital. Another volume of the same type as the works mentioned above appeared at New York in 1936, entitled *Geography of Latin America* by Fred A. Carlson (b.1892). It is of considerable value to historians of economic affairs.

An important work dealing with the rise, spread, and decline of the American Indian appeared in 1927 at New York under the title *The story of the American Indian.* The author was the well-known anthropologist Paul Radin (b.1883). The book appeared in a new edition at New York in 1934.

In 1927, also, a specialized study appeared entitled *The Spanish American frontier 1783-1795; the westward movement and the Spanish retreat in the Mississippi Valley* (Boston). The author was Arthur P. Whitaker (b.1895).

A work dealing with the relations of Europe and Hispanic America was published in 1928 at New York under the title *Latin America in world politics* and written by J. Fred Rippy. In the same year Alfred Hasbrouck brought out through the Columbia University Press his misentitled *Foreign legionaries in the liberation of Spanish South America,* written as a doctoral dissertation.

A work of value to the cultural and literary historian is *Some Spanish American poets* (New York, 1929) by Alice Stone Blackwell (b.1857). A second printing of this work appeared at Philadelphia in 1937.

In 1930 at London the Hakluyt Society (Volume LXV, second series) published the first of four contemplated volumes by Cecil Jane (1879-1932) entitled *Select documents illustrating the four voyages of Columbus,* which contained a brilliant introductory essay concerning the historical setting of the voyages and the psychological make-up of the discoverer. This work had been preceded by his brief and thought-provoking *Liberty and despotism in Spanish America* (Oxford, 1929).

In 1930, also, a collection of biographies of value to the historian of the Spanish period in Florida was published at New York by the United States Catholic Historical Society under the title *Dominicans in early Florida.* The author was the Very Rev. Victor Francis O'Daniel (b.1868).

In 1931 Waldo Frank (b.1889) published his popular volume entitled *America Hispana* (reissued at New York in 1940 as *South of us*), which aimed to interpret the history and social and economic life of Hispanic America. In the same year appeared at New York and London a highly specialized and scholarly volume by Philip Ainsworth Means (b.1892) entitled *Ancient civilizations of the Andes.*

In 1933 The George Washington University Press began, under the editorship of A. Curtis Wilgus, the publication of works dealing with Latin America. The first volume bore the title *Modern Hispanic America* and was published at Washington, D. C. The next year a second volume, entitled *The Caribbean area,* was issued. In 1935 a third volume appeared with the title *Argentina, Brazil, and Chile since independence;* in 1936 a fourth volume was published, entitled *Colonial Hispanic America;* and in 1937 at Washington appeared the fifth and final volume in the series, entitled *South American dictators.* Each volume contained a series of lectures given by experts in the field before the Seminar Conference on Hispanic American Affairs held under the auspices of the Center of Inter-American Studies.

A book, long needed, concerning Portuguese explorations appeared in 1933 under the title *The Portuguese pioneers.* It was written by Edgar Prestage (b.1869) and was published at London as part of *The pioneer histories,* edited by V. T. Harlow (b.1898) and F. A. Williamson. Of outstanding importance for the student of Hispanic America are three other volumes in this series: *The explorers of North America, 1492-1806,* by J. B. Brebner (b.1895), New York, 1933; *The Spanish conquistadores,* by F. A. Kirkpatrick (b.1861), London, 1934; and *The European nations in the West Indies, 1493-1688,* by Arthur Percival Newton (b.1873), London, 1933. In 1933 appeared the excellent synthesis by Charles E. Chapman (1880-1941) entitled *Colonial Hispanic America, a history* (New York, 1933), which is intended for a textbook. A second volume, *Republican Hispanic America: a history,* followed at New York in 1937.

A highly important work of a specialized nature appeared during 1934 at Chapel Hill, under the title *Church and state in Latin America.* The author was J. Lloyd Mecham (b.1893) of the University of Texas. During this year also were published the following books of value to the historian of Hispanic American life and civilization: *Education in Latin America* (New York) by Henry Lester Smith (b.1876) and Harold Littell; *Latin American music, past and present* (Santa Ana, California) by Eleanore Hague; *Ores and industry in South America* (New York) by H. Foster Bain (b.1872) and Thomas T. Read (b.1880); and *American treasure and the price revolution in Spain, 1501 to 1650* (Cambridge, Mass.) by Earl Jefferson Hamilton (b.1899).

In 1935 appeared a very useful work by Philip Ainsworth Means entitled *The Spanish main, focus of envy, 1492-1700* (New York). In the same year John Tate Lanning published at Chapel Hill his study of the *Spanish missions in Georgia.*

In 1936 appeared a much-needed study of Spanish missions and missionaries in South America. It was entitled *Crusaders of the jungle* (Chapel Hill) and was the joint work of J. Fred Rippy and Jean Thomas Nelson. Another work appearing in this year of value to the historian is *Ancient life in Mexico and Central America* (Indianapolis) by Edgar Lee Hewett (b.1865).

In 1937 several books appeared in English of special interest for the historian of Hispanic America. Among these were *The Franciscan conquest of Florida (1573-1618)* by Rev. Maynard Geiger, published at Washington, D. C., as a doctoral dissertation; *Latin America, its place in world life* (Chicago), an interpretation of contemporary Híspanic American civilization by Samuel Guy Inman (b.1877), the well-known American writer and lecturer; *America south* (Philadelphia) by the journalist and traveler Carleton Beals (b.1893), who had already written widely on Hispanic American topics; and *The republics of South America* (London, 1937), a convenient economic treatise prepared by a study group of members of the Royal Institute of International Affairs in London.

The most extensive work in English of a scholarly type is *The rise of the Spanish Empire in the old world and in the new* (4 vols., New York, 1918-34), by Roger Bigelow Merriman (b.1876).

2. *In Foreign Languages*

Among the general works in languages other than English which deal with Hispanic America are many of considerable value. Doubtless the best known is that by the Mexican historian, Carlos Pereyra (b.1871), entitled *Historia de América española* and published at Madrid in eight volumes between 1920 and 1926. Two extensive general works dealing with the Spanish American colonies and with the mother country appeared about the same time. The first was published at Barcelona before 1920 (the date is not known) in twenty-five volumes under the title of *Historia de España y de las repúblicas latinoamericanas.* The author was Alfredo Opisso (b.1847). The second work was the twenty-three-volume *Historia de América y de los pueblos americanos.* The general editor is the well-known Spanish historian, Antonio Ballesteros Beretta. Volume I appeared in 1936 at Barcelona under the title *América indígena* by Luis Pericot García.

From 1902 to 1923 at Berlin appeared Eduard Seler's (1849-1922) great work entitled *Gesammelte abhandlungen zur amerikanischen sprach und alterthumskunde,* which constitutes an exhaustive treatment of Mexican and Mayan life and speech with some discussion of the Incas. Many other important works have come from the pen of this great scholar.

Between 1904 and 1913 appeared at Madrid the four-volume *Los pueblos hispano-americanos en el siglo XX* by Ricardo Beltrán y Rózpide (b.1852). This covered the period from 1901 to 1912. A brief one-volume edition of 748 pages appeared at Madrid in 1930.

In 1908 at Santiago, Chile, José Toribio Medina (1852-1930) brought out in two volumes his *El veneciano Sebastián Caboto,* which sketches the lives of the explorer and his companions and reproduces many important documents. In the same year appeared at Santiago his *Algunas noticias de León Pancaldo,* who attempted to reach Peru by way of the Strait of Magellan, *El portugués Esteban Gómez al servicio de España,* and *Los viajes de Diego García de Moguer al Río de la Plata.* Among his other important works of a historical nature are *El descubrimiento del Océano Pacífico* (4 vols., Santiago, 1913-20); *La primitiva inquisición americana* (2 vols., Santiago, 1914); *El piloto Juan Fernández* (Santiago, 1918); *Bartolomé Ruiz de Andrada, primer piloto del mar del sur* (Santiago, 1919); and the innumerable and invaluable histories of the press and printing in various parts of Hispanic America.

Between 1908 and 1916 there was published at Santiago, Chile, the sixteen-volume *Obras completas* of the revered historian Diego Barros Arana, who died in 1907. These volumes contained his historical writings.

Between 1910 and 1913 at Buenos Aires Carlos Navarro y Lamarca's *Compendio de la historia general de América* was published in two profusely illustrated volumes. In 1912 there appeared the first of seven volumes at Madrid entitled *Historia de la Compañía de Jesús de la asistencia de España* by Antonio Astraín (b.1857). The last volume was published in 1925. The whole work contains much valuable information about the Jesuits in America.

In 1917 Juan Ortega y Rubio (b.1845) brought out at Madrid his illustrated *Historia de América* in three volumes, giving the history from the earliest times to the present.

During the years 1918 to 1920 at Buenos Aires was published posthumously the *Historia diplomática latino-americana* in three volumes by Vicente Gaspar Quesada (1830-1913). This work had been preceded by other volumes of historical importance, notably his *La Vida intelectual en la América española durante los siglos XVI, XVII y XVIII* (Buenos Aires, 1910), the *Derecho público eclesiástico* (Buenos Aires, 1910), the *Historia colonial argentina* (Buenos Aires, 1915), and others.

In 1927 appeared at Buenos Aires in two volumes the *Nacimiento de las repúblicas americanas* by the prolific historical writer Gonzalo Bulnes (1851-1936), whose *Bolívar en el Perú* (2 vols., Madrid, 1919) and whose works on the War of the Pacific had won him international fame. Two years later, at Paris, Jean Toussaint Bertrand brought out his two-volume *Histoire de l'Amérique espagnole,* which traced the history of Hispanic America from the earliest times.

Two geographical works valuable for the historian appeared at Paris in the important collection, *Géographie universelle,* edited by Paul Vidal de la Blache (1845-1918) and L. Gallois. The first work bore the title *Amérique du Sud* and was published at Paris, two volumes in one, as Volume XV of the series. The author was Pierre Denis. The second work, entitled *Mexique —Amérique Centrale,* was Volume XIV of the series (Paris, 1928). The author was Maximilien Sorre.

Among the shorter works of a general nature the following should be cited. In 1909 the *Elementos de historia contemporánea de América* by Emilio Vera y González was published at Buenos Aires in one volume. In 1911 Ernst Robert Daenell (b.1872) published in Munich and Berlin *Die Spanier in Nordamerika, 1513-1824.*

In 1912 at Madrid appeared Rafael María de Labra y Cadrana's (1843-1919) *España y América 1812-1912,* tracing international and constitutional relations between the two regions. This work was followed at Madrid in the same year by his *América y la constitución española de 1812.* Also in 1912 at Paris Carlos A. Villanueva (b.1865) brought out his two-volume *La monarquía en América,* which dealt with Bolívar and San Martín, and the relations between Fernando VII and the new states. The next year at Paris appeared his one-volume *Resumen de la historia general de América.* In 1912 at Berlin and Leipzig there appeared the first volume of the *Geschichte Sudamerika* by Hermann A. L. Lufft (b.1880). In 1913 Francisco García Calderón published at Paris *La creación de un continente,* dealing with Pan Americanism, Iberianism, and society in Hispanic America.

In 1912 at Leipzig and Paris Erland Nordenskiöld (b.1877), an archaeologist and ethnologist, published his study on the Indians of the Gran Chaco. The French volume bore the title *La vie des indiens dans le Chaco.* From 1919 to 1922 appeared at Göteborg four volumes of his *Comparative ethnological studies* translated from the original German edition of 1918. This work deals with the South American Indians in general and with the Indians of the Gran Chaco in particular. Many other valuable studies have been written by this author.

In 1917 there appeared at Barcelona the comprehensive but diffuse *Historia del comercio con las indias durante el dominio de los Austrias* by Gervasio de Artiñano y de Galdácano. This work was followed in 1920 at Madrid by his *La arquitectura naval española.*

In 1920 at Madrid was published a scholarly and documentary two-volume work, valuable for an account of the discovery and exploration of the Strait of Magellan, by the Jesuit Pablo Pastells (b.1846) under the title *El descubrimiento del Estrecho de Magallanes.*

In 1922 Rufino Blanco-Fombona (b.1874) brought out at Madrid his interpretative essay entitled *El conquistador español del siglo XVI.* This had been preceded by numerous other works of a literary and historical nature, of which his brief *La evolución política y social de Hispano-América* (Madrid, 1911) should be especially mentioned.

In the nineteen twenties—the exact year is unknown—José Vasconcelos (b.1882) of Mexico published a most thought-provoking book under the title *La raza cósmica, misión de la raza iberoamericana; notas de viajes en la América del Sur.* The volume appeared at Paris and dealt largely with Argentina and Brazil. In 1937 at Mexico City appeared this author's *Breve historia de México* in a third edition covering the subject from pre-Columbian times to about 1930.

In 1926 José R. del Franco published at Madrid his excellent *Nociones de geografía é historia de América,* which deals with the whole continent and which contains much valuable material for historians. The next year Pedro Aguado Bleye (b.1884) brought out at Bilbao his *Manual de historia de América,* which appeared in a third enlarged edition two years later at the same place. In 1927 *El nacimiento de la América española* appeared at Tucumán. The author was Juan Bautista Terán (1880-1938). A French translation appeared at Paris in 1930 and an Italian translation was published at Bari in 1931. The book deals with Spanish America to 1600.

In 1928 a German work written by Karl Heinrich Panhorst and entitled *Deutschland und Amerika* appeared at München. The book dealt with Germans in America before 1600 and particularly with the Fuggers and the Welsers. In 1928 also the Peruvian historian Jorge Guillermo Leguía (1898-1934) brought out at Lima the first volume of his *Historia de América,* a text for colleges and secondary schools.

In 1929 at Madrid Enrique de Gandía (b.1906) brought out his interesting one-volume work on the *Historia crítica de los mitos de la conquista americana.* In the same year at Madrid also appeared the comprehensive summary entitled *Compendio de geografía, historia y constituciones de América* by Francisco de Arce, while in the same year at Zaragoza appeared the brief essay on *España en América* by Juan Fernández Amador de Los Ríos.

The year following at Madrid Carlos Pereyra (b.1871) published his one-volume *Breve historia de América,* and in the same year (1930) at the same place appeared the brief *Historia moderna de la América española* by Ciro Bayo (b.1860), covering the period since independence, from the Spanish point of view. In 1930 at Leipzig appeared a general work dealing with commercial and economic conditions in Hispanic America entitled *Lateinamerika* by Hermann A. L. Lufft.

In 1931 at Madrid was published the *Historia de España en América* by an Ecuadorian, Nicolás Espinosa Cordero (b.1902), which dealt with the pre-Columbian and colonial periods. Also in 1931 Adolf Rein (b.1885) brought out an excellent comprehensive essay on geographical discoveries, colonization, and world politics which treats the Spanish colonial system. The book bears the title *Die europäische ausbreitung über die erde* and contains 262 text illustrations and 22 plates. It was published at Potsdam.

The next year (1932) at Leipzig the geographer Oscar Schmieder (b.1891) published a historical geography describing the evolution of South American areas under the title *Länderkunde Südamerikas.* The same year Alfredo Colmo (b.1878) published at Buenos Aires his *La revolución en la América latina.*

In 1933 the well-known American writer and lecturer, Samuel Guy Inman, brought out at Madrid his thoughtful discussions on Hispanic American society, economics, and politics entitled *América revolutionaria, conferencias y ensayos.*

In 1935 Miguel Solá, of the School of Fine Arts at Buenos Aires, published a valuable study dealing with the sixteenth, seventeenth, and eighteenth centuries and entitled *Historia del arte hispano-americana* . . . at Barcelona. The next year at the same place appeared his *Historia de arte precolumbiana.*

In 1936 Octavio Méndez Pereira (b.1887), the well-known Panama author and educator, brought out his brief *Historia de Ibero-América* written for the middle grades. The book was published at Panama City. In the same year at Paris was published the *Histoire de l'Amérique espagnole,* by Hugo David Barbagelata (b.1886), the author of numerous works on South American literature and the revolutionary period. Also in 1936 at Berlin appeared the *Geographie und geschichte der Indianischen landwirschaft* by Karl Sapper (b.1886), the author of many works on American archaeology, anthropology, geography, and allied fields.

In 1938 at Bogotá the Columbian historian Luis Cuervo Márquez brought out in two volumes his important study entitled *Independencia de las colonias hispano-americanas. Participación de la Gran Bretaña y de los Estados Unidos.* In the same year a cooperative work entitled *Historia de la música latino-americana* (Buenos Aires) was prepared by Rolando V. García and others. In 1940 appeared at Buenos Aires the invaluable work *El libro, la imprenta y el periodismo en América durante la dominación española* by José Torre Revello (b.1893). This was followed the same year at the same place by his *Origines de la imprenta en España y su desarrollo en América española.* In 1940 also was published at Montevideo the *Movimientos revolutionarios en las colonias españolas de América* by Lincoln Machado Ribas. In 1941 the brief *El estado español en las Indias* was printed at Mexico City, the author being José María Ots Capdequi.

C. Works on Individual Countries and Regions

1. *Brazil*

Several important works dealing with Brazil should be cited. The most extensive treatise was published in ten volumes at Rio de Janeiro in 1905 under the title *Historia do Brasil.* The author was José Francisco da Rocha Pombo (b.1857), whose work is indispensable to the student of Brazilian history. Another work with the same title, *Historia do Brasil,* appeared in five volumes at São Paulo between 1910 and 1913. The author was Raphael Maria Galanti.

A work of value to all writers on Brazil is the four-volume *Livro do centenario, 1500-1900,* published at Rio de Janeiro from 1900 to 1902 by the Association for the Fourth Centenary of the Discovery of Brazil. This contains contributions from many leading Brazilian scholars.

One of the most widely known of Brazilian historians was Manoel de Oliveira Lima (1865-1928), who in 1901 at Rio de Janeiro published his *Historia diplomatica do Brasil.* Two of his brief but important works consist of published lectures. In 1911 he published at Paris a series of lectures delivered at the Sorbonne under the title *Formation historique de la nationalité brésilienne.* This was reprinted in Spanish and published at Madrid in 1918. In 1914 a series of lectures delivered at Stanford University was printed by the University under the title *The evolution of Brazil compared with Spanish and Anglo-Saxon America.* This was also translated into Spanish and published at Madrid in 1919. A larger work of great value is *Dom João no Brasil, 1808-1821* (2 vols., Rio de Janeiro, 1908). Two briefer studies are his *O movimento da independencia, 1821-1822* (São Paulo, 1922), and his *O império brasileiro, 1822-1889* (São Paulo, 1927).

In 1902 at Rio de Janeiro Euclydes da Cunha (1866-1909) published his study of the *campanha de canudos* entitled *Os Sertões* which has been revised and reissued in nearly a dozen subsequent editions.

In 1904 appeared at Rio de Janeiro an important treatise entitled *Religiões acatholicas no Brasil, 1500-1900,* by José Carlos Rodrigues (1844-1922).

In 1906 there was published at Rio de Janeiro the first volume of the *Historia territorial do Brasil* written by Felisbello Firmo de Oliveira Freire. The next year the first volume of his *Os Portuguezes no Brasil* was printed at the same place. In 1912 José Manoel Cardoso de Oliveira brought out at Rio de Janeiro a two-volume work which he edited and which was entitled *Actos diplomaticos do Brasil. . . .* In the same year appeared a work of value to the student of Portuguese backgrounds entitled *L'astronomie nautique au Portugal à l'époque des grandes découvertes.* The volume appeared at Bern; a new edition was published at Geneva in 1917. The author was Joaquim Bensaude. Another valuable work by the same author bore the title *Histoire de la science nautique portugaise* (7 vols., Munich, 1914 or 1915). This contains a collection of documents, illustrations, tables, and the like, which was published at the instigation of the Portuguese government.

In 1914 at Bogotá in Colombia appeared *El Brazil á través de su historia* by Gustavo Arboleda R. (b.1881).

In 1915 at Rio de Janeiro Basilio de Magalhães (b.1874) brought out the first edition of his important *Expansão geographica do Brasil colonial,* dealing with territorial expansion in the colony. A new augmented second edition with the title changed slightly was published at São Paulo in 1935.

In 1920 at Buenos Aires appeared posthumously *La politica imperialistica del Brazil* by the Argentine writer, Vicente Gaspar Quesada.

In 1921 was published at O'Porto the first volume of the monumental *Historia da colonização portuguesa do Brasil,* compiled under the direction of Carlos Malheiro Dias. The third volume appeared in 1923 at the same place. In 1921, also, there appeared the *Queda do imperio* by Ruy Barbosa (1849-1923), which dealt with the transition period from empire to republic. It was published at Rio de Janeiro in two volumes. Also in 1921 was published at Rio de Janeiro the widely used school history of Brazil by

Mario Vasconcellos Veiga Cabral (b.1894), entitled *Compendio de historia do Brasil.*

The history of music in Brazil is told in Italian in the excellent work entitled *Storia dela musica nel Brasile . . .* by Vincenzo Cernicchiaro. It was published in 1923 at Milan.

In 1927 and 1928 appeared the two-volume *A politica exterior do império* by João Pandiá Calogeras (1870-1934), which was printed at Rio de Janeiro. Two years later, in 1930, at Rio de Janeiro the same author brought out his *Formação historica do Brasil,* first published as a series of lectures the previous year. In 1939 this volume was brought out by the University of North Carolina Press in an eighth edition translated and edited by P. A. Martin with the title *A History of Brazil.* In 1930 at Rio de Janeiro was published *O Brasil na America* by Manoel José do Bomfim (b.1868), which dealt with the foundation of Brazil, and *O descobrimento do Brasil* by João Capistrano de Abreu (1853-1927), one of the leading Brazilian historians. Both of these men have written numerous other works on Brazilian history. In 1929 appeared at São Paulo the interesting *Historias que não vêm na historia* by F. Assis Cintra. This had been preceded by his *D. Pedro I e o grito da independencia* (São Paulo, 1921) and *Tiradentes perante a historia* (São Paulo, 1922).

In 1931 at Barcelona appeared an excellent historical summary by Gonzalo de Reparaz (b.1860) entitled *La época de los grandes descubrimientos españoles y portugueses,* while in the same year, at Rio de Janeiro, Jonathas Serrano (b.1885) brought out his valuable illustrated one-volume *Historia do Brasil* as a textbook for secondary schools.

In 1932 at Rio de Janeiro appeared the important and profusely illustrated *O Rio de Janeiro no tempo dos vice-reis, 1763-1808,* by Luiz Edmundo. This work was translated into English by Dorothea H. Momsen and published in 1936 at Rio de Janeiro.

In 1933 Pedro Calmon Moniz de Bittencourt (b.1902) published his *Historia de civilização bresileira* at São Paulo (translated into Spanish at Buenos Aires, 1937). This had been preceded by several other works, including his *Historia da independencia do Brasil* (Rio de Janeiro, 1928), and it was followed by his *Espirito da sociedade colonial* (São Paulo, 1935), his *Historia diplomatica do Brasil* (Rio de Janeiro?, 1939), and other works.

In 1933, also, Max Fleiuss (b.1868) brought out at Rio de Janeiro his *Apostilas de historia do Brasil* as a special volume published by the Instituto Historico e Geographico Brasileiro. This comprises a series of valuable essays which give an outline of Brazilian history. In this connection attention should be called to the *Diccionario historico, geographico e ethnographico do Brasil,* a work indispensable to the student of Brazilian history which is being brought out by the Instituto. The first two volumes appeared at Rio de Janeiro in 1922.

A book of great value for the historian of Brazilian colonial life and customs is by the sociologist Gilberto Freyre. It was published at Rio de Janeiro in 1933 under the title *Casa-grande e Senzala; formação da familia brasileira sob o regimen de economia patriarchal* and contains some four hundred pages. A second edition appeared in the same place in 1936.

An important comprehensive work for historians which appeared in two volumes at São Paulo in 1937 is *Historia economica do Brasil 1500-1820,* by Roberto Cochrane Simonsen (b.1889). In 1937, also, Professor Annibal Mattos (b.1889) published two volumes of his excellent and invaluable *Historia da arte brasileira* at Bello Horizonte as Volume XII of *Bibliotheca Mineira de Cultura.* In 1938 at Lisbon there appeared the two-volume complete and documented *Historia da companhia de Jesus no Brasil* by Serafim Leite. In the same year appeared at São Paulo *O dominio colonial hollandez no Brasil,* a translation of an important work printed in Heidelberg (?) in 1921 by Hermann Watjen. Also in 1938 appeared a revised and enlarged edition of the *Historia Monetaria do Brasil colonial* (Rio de Janeiro) by Severino Sombra. At São Paulo in 1940 Afranio Peixoto (b.1876) brought out his ambitious *Pequena historia das Americas,* while in the same year at Porto he published his *Historia do Brasil.*

Among the works of this century written in English about Brazil are *The new Brazil* (Philadelphia, 1901), a descriptive and historical volume by Marie R. Wright (b.1866); *North Brazil and South Brazil,* by E. Charles Buley (2 vols., London, 1914); *Brazil and her people today* (Boston, 1909, and subsequent editions), by Nevin Otto Winter (b.1869); *The United States of Brazil,* by C. W. Domville-Fife, published at London in 1910; *Among the wild tribes of the Amazons,* published at Philadelphia in 1924 by the same author; *Brazil,* by Pierre Denis, printed in English at London in 1911 (a translation from the French at Paris in 1909); *Brazil of today and tomorrow* by Lilian Elwyn Elliott, which appeared at New York in 1922; *The constitutional system of Brazil* (Washington, D. C., 1923) and *Brazil after a century of independence* (London, 1925) by H. G. James; *The conquest of Brazil* (New York, 1926) by Roy Nash, which deals with modern conditions; *Brazil. A study in economic types* (Chapel Hill, N. C., 1935), written in 1932, by J. F. Normano; and *Dom Pedro the magnanimous* (Chapel Hill, N. C., 1937) by Mary W. Williams.

2. *Mexico*

A number of important works dealing with Mexico have appeared in this century. From 1900 to 1902 at Mexico City appeared a work in three volumes edited by Justo Sierra (1848-1912) under the title *México, su evolución social.* An English edition appeared in two volumes in three at Mexico City, 1900-04. This work constitutes a veritable handbook of Mexican affairs.

In 1901 at Mexico City, one of the great Mexican scholars, Genaro García (1867-1920), widely known for his editing of innumerable historical works, brought out the *Carácter de la conquista española en América y en México según los textos de los historiadores primitivos*. In 1906 at Mexico City he published *La inquisición de México* from a collection of manuscripts preserved in the National Museum of Mexico. This study was Volume V of an exceedingly valuable collection of documents entitled *Documentos inéditos ó muy raros para la historia de México* (35 vols., Mexico, 1905-11) which García and Carlos Pereyra (b.1871) edited jointly.

In 1902 Nicolás León (1859-1929) brought out at Mexico City his *Compendio de historia general de México,* covering Mexican history from the earliest times to 1900. An improved second edition appeared at Mexico City in 1919. In 1902 there was printed at Mexico City the first volume of this author's *Bibliografía mexicana en el siglo XIX.*

In 1903 Roland Bonaparte (1858-1924) and others brought out at Paris the two-volume *Le Mexique au début du XX siècle.* Two years later, in 1905, at Santiago, Chile, José Toribio Medina published his *Historia del tribunal del santo oficio de la inquisición en México.*

In 1907 at Philadelphia Alcée Fortier (1856-1914) and John Rose Ficklen published their *Central America and Mexico* as Volume IX of the "History of North America" series, edited by G. C. Lee (b.1862) and F. N. Thorpe (b.1857), twenty volumes, published at Philadelphia from 1903 to 1907.

In 1907 also Nevin Otto Winter brought out at Boston his *Mexico and her people today* of which later editions were issued.

In 1908 at San Francisco appeared the first volume of Father Zephyrin Engelhardt's (b.1851) invaluable treatise on *The missions and missionaries of California.* The work was completed in four volumes at the same place in 1915, while an index volume appeared the next year. A new edition of the work began to appear at Santa Barbara in 1929. Father Engelhardt is the author of many special treatises on individual California missions, and his work is invaluable for the student of Spanish missions.

Another extensive work begun in 1908 was entitled *Ciudades coloniales y capitales de la república mexicana* (4 vols., Mexico, 1908-11). The author was Antonio Peñafiel (1831-1921) and his study was limited to 200 printed copies.

In 1909 W. H. Koebel (1872-1923) published his one-volume *Mexico* at London and C. R. Enock brought out at the same place his single volume under the same title. In this year, also, at Mexico City appeared the two-volume *Historia del pueblo mejicano* by Carlos Pereyra, which dealt with the political organization of the country. The year following Alberto Leduc published at Mexico City his large and valuable *Diccionario de geografía, historia y biografía mexicanas.*

In 1911 at Paris, Maurice, Comte de Périgny (b.1877), brought out his *Les états-unis du Mexique.*

In 1916 Enrique Santibáñez (b.1869) published at Mexico City his *Estudios de historia nacional contemporánea.* This was followed in 1923 at Mexico City by his *Historia nacional de México,* dealing with the period from the earliest times to the present. In 1916 also Manuel Romero de Terreros y Vinent (b.1880) brought out his important *Arte colonial* at Mexico City. This was followed by a second volume (Mexico, 1918) and by a third volume (Mexico, 1921) bearing the same title. In 1923 at the same place appeared his *Las artes industriales en la Nueva España* dealing with colonial industry, trade, and art in New Spain. In 1925 at New York, in collaboration with Solomon Leopold Millard Rosenberg (b.1869), he published *México; virreinal acuarelas de Nueva España,* dealing with colonial life, customs, art, and the like. Many other works have come from this author's pen.

In 1920 appeared at both Mexico City and Paris *La evolución histórica de México* by Emilio Rabasa (b.1856). The next year *México hacia el fin del virreinato español* by Gregorio Torres Quintero was published at Mexico City. In 1921 also appeared Volume I of the *Historia de la iglesia en México* at Mexico City by P. Mariano Cuevas (b.1879). The whole work in five volumes was finally published at El Paso, Texas, in 1928. The period treated is from 1511 to 1910. This treatise had been preceded by two others of value edited by the same author: *Documentos inéditos del siglo XVI para la historia de México* (Mexico, 1914), and *Cartas y otros documentos de Hernán Cortés* (Sevilla, 1915). In 1940 at Mexico City he brought out his large *Historia de la nación mexicana* with 550 illustrations.

In 1923 at Madrid was printed the very useful two-volume biographical dictionary compiled by Francisco A. de Icaza (b.1863) under the title *Conquistadores y pobladores de Nueva España.* The same year the best one-volume history in English concerning Mexico was published at New York under the title *The Mexican Nation.* The author was Herbert I. Priestley (b.1875). Also in 1923 at Mexico City appeared the first edition of Jesús Romero Flores' *Historia de la civilización mexicana.* An earlier work by the same author had appeared at Mexico City under the title *Páginas de historia.*

From 1921 to 1928 appeared at Mexico City in four volumes in two the *Historia de México desde la restauración de la república en 1867 hasta la caída de Porfirio Díaz* by R. García Granados. In 1923 George McCutchen McBride published at New York his valuable and detached work on *The land systems of Mexico,* which had been written as a doctoral dissertation at Yale.

An important publication begun in 1923 and completed in a third volume in 1937 (Washington, D.C.) was edited by Charles Wilson Hackett (b.1888) under the title *Historical documents relating to New Mexico,*

Nueva Vizcaya and approaches thereto to 1773, which had been collected by F. A. and Fanny R. Bandelier. The text is in Spanish and English translations.

In 1924 appeared at Vienna in two volumes *Maximilian und Charlotta von Mexico* by Egon Caesar Corti (b.1886). An English translation was published in two volumes at New York and London in 1928 under the same title.

A work of great use to historians is the *Geografía de la república mexicana* (2 vols., Mexico, 1926-27), written by the author of more than eighty other works in various fields, Jesús Galindo y Villa (1867-1937).

In 1926 at Mexico City Alfonso Toro (b.1873) brought out in three volumes his *Compendio de historia de México,* which covered the period from earliest times to the present. A third edition appeared at Mexico City in 1938. In 1926, also, Wilfred Hardy Callcott (b.1895) published his important *Church and state in Mexico, 1822-1857,* at Durham, N. C. This was followed by a second volume published at Stanford University in 1931 under the title *Liberalism in Mexico, 1857-1917.* In 1926, also, Ernest Gruening (b.1887) brought out at New York his comprehensive *Mexico and its heritage.* This appeared in a new edition in 1930.

In 1929 through the University of California Press at Berkeley Lesley Byrd Simpson (b.1891) brought out his study, *The encomienda in New Spain,* and in 1934 at the same place his *Studies in the administration of the Indians in New Spain.*

In 1930 at Durham, Charles S. Braden published his *Religious aspects of the conquest of Mexico.* Three years later at Paris appeared a work on the same subject by Robert Ricard entitled *La Conquête spirituelle du Mexique,* which shows the methods and measures of the conquest from 1523 to 1572. A work of special value to the social historian is the *Historia del teatro principal de México* (Mexico, 1932) by Manuel Mañón. In 1934 at Mexico City appeared Volume I of the *Historia de México,* covering the period before Cortés and written by Luis Chávez Orozco. This was reissued in 1939. In 1934 also Julio Jiménez Rueda (b.1896) published his revised *Historia de la literatura mexicana* at Mexico City. This had first appeared there in 1928.

A work of great value to students in the United States is entitled *Guide to the history of Mexico* (Mexico, 1935) by Alfonso Teja Zabre (b.1888). In 1935 also at Mexico City José López-Portillo y Weber published his *La conquista de la Nueva Galicia,* containing an excellent collection of colonial maps.

In 1936 the portion of New Spain called Texas was treated by Carlos E. Castañeda (b.1896) in two volumes on *The mission era* published at Austin. The first volume bore the subtitle *The finding of Texas* and the second volume *The winning of Texas.* Volumes III and IV appeared in 1938 and 1939, respectively. This is part of a larger work of seven volumes, to be called

Our Catholic heritage in Texas, 1519-1936, which is sponsored by the Texas Knights of Columbus Historical Commission.

In 1937 Volume I of *Apuntes para la historia del derecho en México* by Toribio Esquivel Obregón (b.1861) was published at Mexico City. Volume II appeared at the same place in 1938.

In 1939 at Mexico City Dr. Silvio Zavala and María Castelo published Volumes I and II of their *Fuentes para la historia del trabajo en Nueva España (1575-1576).* In the same year also at Mexico City a valuable work for the historian appeared under the title *Tres siglos de pintura colonial mexicana,* by Agustín Velázquez Chávez. Another valuable work published during this year was *Los Franciscanos y la imprenta en México en el siglo XVI* (Mexico, 1939) by Román Zulaica Garate. Other recent works are *Historia de la Ciudad de México* (Mexico, 1939) by Artemio de Valle-Arizpe (b.1888); *Epistolario de Nueva España, 1505-1818* (6 vols., Mexico, 1939; 2 vols., Mexico, 1940), a collection of documents of great value for the historian compiled by Francisco del Paso y Troncoso (1842-1916); *Fiestas y costumbres mexicanas* (Volume I, Mexico, 1940) by Higinio Vásquez Santa Ana; *Historia de México* (Volume III at Mexico, 1940) by Francisco Banegas Galván, who brought out Volume II in 1923; and *La obra de los Jesuitas mexicanas durante le época colonial, 1572-1767* (2 vols., Mexico, 1941) by Gerardo Decorme.

3. *Spanish Florida*

Interest in the early history of Florida was renewed in this century by the Florida State Historical Society, which began the publication of a number of historical documents relating to the early history of the region under the able editorship of James Alexander Robertson (1873-1939). Mrs. Jeannette Thurber Connor brought out *Colonial records of Spanish Florida* at Deland in two volumes, the first appearing in 1925 and the second in 1930. Volume I covered the period 1570 to 1577, and Volume II the period from 1577 to 1580. Mrs. Connor's untimely death was a great blow to the organization. In 1931 at Deland Arthur Preston Whitaker published his volume entitled *Documents relating to the commercial policy of Spain in the Floridas, with incidental reference to Louisiana.* Among other works published by the Society is *The Luna papers . . . ,* translated and edited by H. I. Priestley (2 vols., Deland, 1928). *The Spanish approach to Pensacola, 1689-93,* which was prepared for the Society by Irving A. Leonard, was finally published by the Quivira Society at Albuquerque, N. M., in 1939.

4. *Central America (Guatemala)*

Among the general works dealing with Central America two in English may be mentioned. In 1914 at New York appeared W. H. Koebel's *Central*

America which was reprinted at London in 1917; D. G. Munro's (b.1892) *The five republics of Central America* was published at New York in 1918. An English work dealing with Guatemala is *Guatemala and her people today* (Boston, 1909) by Nevin Otto Winter.

In Spanish several works may be cited. In 1915 there appeared at Guatemala City the first volume of a series entitled *La América Central ante la historia* by Antonio Batres Jáuregui (b.1847). In the same year J. Antonio Villacorta (b.1879) brought out his *Curso de historia de la América Central* (Guatemala City, 1915) for use particularly in normal schools. This work was followed in 1922 by his *Elementos de historia patria* in two volumes at Guatemala City. In 1927 the same author, together with Carlos A. Villacorta, brought out the *Arqueología guatemalteca.* This study was followed in 1938 at Guatemala City by the *Prehistoria e historia antigua de Guatemala* by J. Antonio and Carlos A. Villacorta. In 1924 the *Vida militar de Centro-América* by Pedro Zamora Castellanos (b.1879) was published at Guatemala City. In 1925 at San José appeared *Nuestra tierra prometida* by Alejandro Alvarado Quirós (b.1876). In 1926 at Guatemala City was printed the second revised and corrected edition of *Geografía de la América Central* (first published at Managua in 1907) by Felipe Neri Fernández. In 1930 at Guatemala City was published the first of a series entitled *Estudios de historia militar de Centro-América* by José N. Rodríguez.

In French at Paris (ca.1911) Maurice, Comte de Périgny, brought out his well illustrated *Les cinq républiques de l'Amérique Centrale. . . .*

5. *Honduras*

In 1927 at San Pedro, Honduras, appeared a volume bearing the title *Bosquejo histórico de Honduras, 1501 á 1921.* The author was Rómulo Enrique Durón y Gamero (b.1865). In 1938 Ernesto Alvarado García published his *La conquista de Honduras* at Tegucigalpa, which covers the years from the discovery to 1824.

6. *Nicaragua*

In Nicaragua Bernardo Portas published at Managua in 1918 his brief *Compendio de la historia de Nicaragua.* Another brief and earlier work is the *Geografía descriptiva e histórica de Nicaragua* published in 1908 at Managua.

7. *Costa Rica*

In Costa Rica one of the most important historians is Ricardo Fernández Guardia (b.1867), who published the following works: *Historia de Costa Rica* (San José, 1905), dealing with the period of discovery and conquest, which was translated into English by H. W. Van Dyke (b.1872) under the title *History of the discovery and conquest of Costa Rica* (New York, 1913); *Crónicas coloniales* (San José, 1921, and a new revised edition, published at San José in 1927 to which four new chapters have been added to the original twenty-three), dealing with the colonial period; and *La independencia y otros episodios* (San José, 1928).

A work of value to the economic historian appeared at San José in 1940 under the title *Compendio de historia económica y hacendaria de Costa Rica.* The author was Tomás Soley Güell (b.1875).

A French work on Costa Rica appeared at Paris in 1918 under the title *La république de Costa Rica.* The author was Maurice, Comte de Périgny.

8. *El Salvador*

A work written from the documents dealing with El Salvador is the *Historia moderna de El Salvador* by Francisco Gavidia (b.1864), published at San Salvador in two volumes in 1917. The title, however, is misleading, for nearly the entire work treats of the period of independence. Another work in two volumes appeared between 1914 and 1917 at San Salvador and is entitled *Historia de El Salvador.* The work of Santiago Ignacio Barberena (1851-1916), it deals with the pre-Columbian and conquest periods.

Among recent works dealing with El Salvador is the *Diccionario históricoenciclopédio de la repúblic de El Salvador* (2 vols., San Salvador, 1927-39) by Miguel Angel García.

9. *Panama*

In Panama Juan B. Sosa published at Panama City in 1911 his *Compendio de historia de Panamá,* which is in reality a textbook for schools and colleges. Two books in English of considerable value are *Old Panama and Castilla del Oro* (Washington, D.C., 1911) by the army physician, Charles L. G. Anderson (b.1863); and *Panama, the creation, destruction, and resurrection,* by the adventurer, engineer, and statesman, Philippe Buneau-Varilla (1859-1940), which was published at London in 1913.

Books dealing with the Panama Canal are numerous. Among the best are *Panama, past and present* (New York, 1913) by Farnam Bishop (b.1886); *Panama: the canal, the country, and the people* (New York, 1911) by Arthur Bullard (b.1879); *Panama and the canal today* (Boston, 1910) by Charles H. A. Forbes-Lindsay (b.1860); *Four centuries of the Panama Canal* (New York, 1906) by Willis Fletcher Johnson (b.1857); *History of the Panama Canal* (Washington, D. C., 1915) by I. E. Bennett (b.1868); *Panama and the canal* (New York, 1914) by W. J. Abbott; *Cádiz to Cathay. The story of the long struggle for a waterway across the American isthmus* (Stanford University, 1940) by Miles P. Du Val, Jr.; *From Panama to Verdun* (Philadelphia, 1940) by Philippe Bunau-Varilla; and *Suez and Panama* (New York, 1940) by André Siegfried.

10. *West Indies (Cuba)*

Works dealing with Cuba are of considerable importance. In 1918 at Havana appeared a three-volume work entitled *Historial de Cuba* by Ricardo V. Rousset, which comprised a local history of the several provinces. In 1920 a five-volume *History of Cuba* by Willis Fletcher Johnson was published at New York. In 1921 at Havana appeared the first volume of *La historia de Cuba* by Ramiro Guerra Sánchez (b.1880) which treated the period from 1492 to 1555. In 1938 the same author published at Havana his *Manual de historia de Cuba,* dealing with economic, social, and political conditions from the time of discovery to 1868.

The early history of Cuba from 1492 to 1586 is well covered by Miss Irene Aloha Wright (b.1879) in a volume entitled *The early history of Cuba* and published at New York in 1916.

The colonial period is treated by Francisco Figueras (b.1853) in his *Cuba y su evolución colonial* (Havana, 1907).

The independence period has been treated by Vidal Morales y Morales (1848-1904) in his *Contribución a la historia de la independencia de Cuba,* published at Havana in 1901. In 1931 was published at Havana the three-volume *Iniciadores y primeros mártires de la revolución cubana* by the same author.

The period since independence is well summarized by Charles E. Chapman in *A history of the Cuban republic,* published at New York in 1927.

The general diplomatic relations of Cuba are treated by Manuel Márquez Sterling (1872-1934) in his *La diplomacia en nuestra historia,* published at Havana in 1909. An important episode in Cuban history and diplomacy is presented by the well-known Cuban scholar, Herminio Portell Vilá (b.1901) in his *Narciso López y su época,* the first volume of which was published at Havana in 1930. In 1938 at Havana the same author brought out the first of four volumes entitled *Historia de Cuba en sus relaciones con los Estados Unidos y España.* Volume II and III were published in 1939 and Volume IV in 1941.

Among the textbooks are the *Nociones de historia de Cuba* (Havana, 1903) by Vidal Morales y Morales and Carlos de la Torre y Huerta (b.1859),—the latter author in the same year revised his *Manual de historia de Cuba;* and the *Historia de Cuba* (Havana, 1925) by Juan Martín Leiseca. In 1938 at Havana the latter author published his history of the Catholic Church in Cuba under the title *Apuntes para la historia eclesiástica de Cuba.* Also in 1938 at Havana Emilio Roig de Leuchsenring (b.1889) brought out the first volume of his excellent study on the *Historia de la Habana* (to 1565).

In 1939 Diego González published in two volumes at Havana, through the Academia de Historia, his *Historia documentada de los movimientos revolucionarios por la independencia de Cuba, 1852-1867.* In the same year also at Havana Emeterio Santiago Santovenia y Echoide (b.1889) brought out his one-volume *Historia de Cuba.* Another volume published during this year at Havana was the *Compendio de historia de Cuba* by Miguel Angel Fonseca.

11. *Dominican Republic*

Chief among the works dealing with the Dominican Republic are the *Historia moderna de la república dominicana* (Santo Domingo, 1906) by José Gabriel García; the *Bosquejo histórico del descubrimiento y conquista de la isla de Santo Domingo* by Casimiro N. da Moya, who brought out the first volume of this work at Santo Domingo in 1913; the *Resumen de historia patria* (Barcelona, 1922) by Bernardo Pichardo; *Naboth's vineyard: The Dominican Republic* (2 vols., New York, 1928) by Sumner Welles (b.1892); *La cultura y las letras coloniales en Santo Domingo* (Buenos Aires, 1936) by Pedro Henríquez Ureña (b.1884); and *Historia de Santo Domingo* by Joaquín Mariano Incháustegui Cabral, of which Volume I appeared at Santiago, Chile, in 1939.

12. *Haiti*

One of the best works in this century on Haiti is by Jacques Nicolas Léger, whose *Haiti, son histoire et ses détracteurs* was published at New York in 1907. The same year an English edition appeared at New York and at Washington, D.C., under the same title translated into English.

Other works of value in French are the *Manuel d'histoire d'Haiti* (Port-au-Prince, 1924 or 1925) by J. C. Dorsainvil (b.1880), who published an enlarged edition at Port-au-Prince in 1934; the *Histoire d'Haiti* by Auguste Magloire, the first volume of which appeared at Port-au-Prince in 1910; *Henri Christophe dans l'histoire d'Haiti* (Paris, 1931) by Vernaind Leconte; the *Précis méthodique d'histoire d'Haiti* (Port-au-Prince, 1935) by François Stanislas Renier Dalencour (b.1880), which covers the history of the country from the discovery to 1930 with a pro-Pétion bias; and *La nation Haitienne* (Paris, 1938) by Dantès Bellegarde (b.1877).

Among the works in English are *The French revolution in Santo Domingo* (New York, 1914) by Theodore Lothrop Stoddard (b.1883); *The Haitian revolution, 1791-1804* (New York, 1914) by Theophilus Gould Steward (b.1843); *Black democracy* (New York, 1928) by H. P. Davis (b.1875); and *Haiti under American control, 1915-1930* (Boston, 1931) by Arthur Chester Millspaugh (b.1883).

13. *Puerto Rico*

The *Historia de Puerto Rico* by Salvador Brau (1837-1912), published at New York in 1904, is of value for the study of that country. A later volume by the same author, and entitled *La colonización de Puerto Rico,* was published at San Juan in 1907. In 1922 at New York appeared the comprehensive *Historia de Puerto Rico* by P. G. Miller (b.1875). In 1930, through the medium of the Brookings Institution in Washington, D.C., Victor S. Clark (b.1868) and his associates brought out a volume on *Porto Rico and its problems* which is of great value to the student of the island.

14. *Colombia*

The following histories concerning Colombia may be mentioned. In 1909 and 1910 there appeared at Bogotá the two-volume *República de Colombia,* written by Soledad Acosta de Samper (1833-1913), which contained a valuable treatment of the independence and modern periods. In the two following years (1911-12) the two-volume *Historia de Colombia* by Jesús María Henao (b.1868) and Gerardo Arrubla (b.1870) was published at Bogotá as a textbook for secondary schools. In 1929 the work was published in a single volume of 811 pages and has been reprinted since. In 1938 Dr. J. Fred Rippy brought out an English edition as a volume in the "Inter-American Historical Series" published at Chapel Hill by the University of North Carolina.

In 1913 P. J. Eder (b.1880) published at New York his summary of Colombian life and affairs in his one-volume *Colombia.*

From 1917 to 1919 at Bogotá appeared the two-volume *Descubrimiento y conquista de Colombia* by Ernesto Restrepo Tirado (b.1862). In 1929 appeared at Sevilla his two-volume *Historia de la provincia de Santa Marta,* while in 1934 at Buenos Aires appeared his brief *Gobernantes del nuevo reino de Granada durante el siglo XVIII.*

Meanwhile in 1918 Gonzalo Uribe Villegas brought out his valuable church history under the title *Los arzobispos y obispos colombianos,* which covers the period from the foundation of the colony to the present; and in 1918 and 1919 Gustavo Arboleda R. published at Bogotá the first two volumes of his *Historia contemporánea de Colombia,* which dealt with the period from 1829 to 1849.

In 1921 appeared the first volume of *El nuevo reino de Granada en el siglo XVIII* (Madrid, 1921) by Jerónimo Bécker (1857-1925) in collaboration with José María Rivas Groot (1864-1923). This work had been preceded at Madrid in 1920 by Bécker's *La política española en las indias,* a comprehensive essay on Spanish colonial policy. In 1923 at Bogotá was published *Los fundadores de Bogotá* by Raimundo Rivas (b.1889), which appeared in a second and revised edition at Bogotá (Vol. I, 1938). In 1926 at Cartagena appeared the first volume of the *Historia moderna colombiana* by Manuel Antonio Pineda C.

In 1928 the first volume of the *Compendio de la historia de Colombia* was published at Bogotá by José Alejandro Bermúdez (1886-1938). In 1934 this work appeared at Bogotá in a third edition completely revised. A fourth edition was printed at the same place in 1937. In 1930 at Guayaquil, Ecuador, was printed the *Proceso histórico de Colombia* by Luis Enrique Navas Prada, which covered the period from the earliest times to 1832. Another work of value to the historian of Colombia is the *Archivo de historia y variedades* (Caracas, 2 vols., 1930-31) by Tulio Febres Cordero (1860-1938).

A volume dealing with relations with the United States appeared at Bogotá in 1926. It was entitled *Colombia y los Estados Unidos de América.* A new and enlarged edition was published in 1931 at the same place. The author was Antonio José Uribe (b.1873), a lawyer and internationalist.

Among recent works are *Las guerras de Bolívar* (5 vols., Bogotá, 1934-40, of which Volumes I and II appeared first at Caracas in 1921-22) by Francisco Rivas Vicuña; and *Historia de la literatura colombiana* (Bogotá, 1938) by Antonio Gómez Restrepo (b.1868).

15. Venezuela

A work dealing with both Colombia and Venezuela appeared at Paris in 1921. The author was Jules Humbert (1867-1935), and the book was entitled *Histoire de la Colombie et du Venezuela des origines jusqu'á nos jours.* This work had been preceded by *Les origines Vénézueliennes,* published at Bordeaux in 1905.

Works dealing entirely with Venezuela are numerous. In 1907 José Gil Fortoul (b.1862) brought out at Berlin his two-volume *Historia constitucional de Venezuela.* This was followed at Madrid in 1916 by his *El hombre y la historia,* which concerned the social history of Venezuela.

Between 1909 and 1911 at Caracas appeared the first ten volumes of the *Historia contemporánea de Venezuela* by Francisco González Guinán (b.1841). In the latter year Lino Duarte Level published at Caracas his *Historia patria,* which covers the history of Venezuela from the conquest through the war of independence. The next year (1912) at London was published the volume entitled *Venezuela* by L. V. Dalton (b.1887). In 1913 the first volume of Bartolomé Tavera Acosta's (b.1865) *A través de la historia de Venezuela* was published at Ciudad Bolívar.

In 1923 at Caracas was published the *Investigaciones históricas* of Vicente Dávila (b.1869), dealing with the colonial period and independence of Venezuela. This was followed the next year by his two-volume *Diccionario biográfico de ilustres próceres de la independencia,* published at Caracas.

More recent works by Venezuelan historians are *Estudios de historia colonial venezolana* (2 vols., Caracas, 1937-38) by Héctor García Chuecos, and his *Historia de la cultura intelectual de Venezuela desde su descubrimiento hasta 1810* (Caracas, 1936); and Volume I of the *Historia de la primera república de Venezuela* (Caracas, 1939) by Carracciolo Parra-Pérez (b.1888), the author of *El régimen español en Venezuela* (Madrid, 1932) and other works on the revolutionary period.

16. Ecuador

Among the chief works concerning Ecuador is the comprehensive *Compendio de historia patria* by Belisario Quevedo (d.1907), which was issued after his death in three volumes at Quito in 1931. Another is *El Ecuador en cien años de independencia, 1830-1930* (2 vols., Quito, 1930) by J. Gonzalo Orellano. Still another extensive and detailed work is the *Historia de la república del Ecuador* by José Le Gouhir y Rodas, the first two volumes of which appeared at Quito in 1920. In 1935 appeared a completely revised edition of Volume I, covering the period from 1822 to 1861. When the study is complete in three volumes, it will treat Ecuadorian history to 1900. Because the author is a French Jesuit, although a resident of Ecuador for more than forty years, his work has caused considerable controversy, yet it should remain one of the most important dealing with the history of the country. A fourth work published at Quito in 1934 is *La historia del Ecuador en la primera mitad del siglo XIX* by Roberto Andrade (b.1851). This historian finally completed his seven-volume *Historia del Ecuador,* which was published at Guayaquil in 1937. Another book, brief but concise, surveys the history of Ecuador from pre-Colombian times to the independence movement. It is entitled *Orígenes de la nacionalidad ecuatoriana* (Quito, 1937). The author is Alberto Múñoz Vernaza (d.1941). A work dealing with the church is *La iglesia ecuatoriana en el siglo XIX* (Quito, 1934) by the religious historian Julio Tobar Donoso (b.1894). The literary historian Alejandro Andrade Coello (b.1886) has written several works of value for the student of Ecuadorian history, including *Motivos nacionales* (2 vols., Quito, 1911-27) and *Crónicas del Quito antiguo* (Quito, 1935).

Several local textbooks concerning the country are entitled *Ecuador: Estudios históricos* (Vol. I, Guayaquil, 1913) and the *Compendio de la historia del Ecuador* (Guayaquil, 1915), both by Camilo Destruge; the *Historia del Ecuador* (2 vols., Quito, 1929-32) by Emilio Uzcátegui García (b.1899); and *Historia de la república . . .* (Quito, 1931) and *Brevíssima historia general del Ecuador* (Quito, 1934) by Oscar Efrén Reyes. The latter work was reissued in augmented form at Quito in 1938.

A brief work of interest on a special subject is *La escultura en el Ecuador* by José Gabriel Navarro, printed at Madrid in 1929. His briefer *El municipio en América durante la existencia de España* (Madrid, 1930) is also of value.

The chief book in English is by C. R. Enock, published at London in 1914 under the title of *Ecuador.*

Among recent works on Ecuador are *El convento de la merced de Quito de 1534-1617* (Quito, 1932; second edition, Quito, 1937) by Joel L. Monroy, which deals with the Mercederians in Ecuador; and *La presidencia de Quito* (2 vols., Quito, 1938-39) by Pío Jaramillo Alvarado.

17. Peru

The largest and most extensive work dealing with Peru published in this century is that by Nemesio Vargas (b.1848) and entitled *Historia del Perú independiente* (8 vols., Lima, 1903-17).

A volume of special nature dealing with the historiography of Peru is entitled *La historia en el Perú,* whose author is José de la Riva Agüero, the younger (b.1885). It was published at Lima in 1910.

Another volume containing important information for the historian is the *Diccionario biográfico de peruanos contemporáneos,* edited by Juan Pedro Paz-Soldán (b.1869) and published at Lima in 1917.

In 1919 appeared Volume I of Pedro Dávilos y Lissón's (b.1863) *La primera centuria.* This work was completed in eight volumes at Lima in 1938. The same author published at Lima in 1931 the first volume of his study on the *Historia republicana del Perú* since 1820. A tenth and final volume appeared at Lima in 1939, at which time Volume I of this same work was reprinted there.

In 1921 at Lima appeared the first volume of Manuel C. Bonilla's study of the period of independence, entitled *Epopeya de la libertad, 1820-1824.* In 1922 at Lima was printed an important work entitled *Historia de las misiones franciscanas . . . del Perú* by Bernardino Izaquierre Ispizua (b.1870), which deals with these missions from 1619 to 1921.

In 1927 at Lima César Antonio Ugarte published his *Bosquejo de la historia económica del Perú,* while in the same year appeared the *Historia internacional y diplomática del Perú* by Arturo García Salazar (b.1886), published in two volumes at Lima.

A though-provoking work for the social historian is the two-volume *La iniciación de la república,* published at Lima in 1928 and 1929. The author is Jorge Basadre (b.1903), librarian and professor of history at the University of San Marcos. In 1937 at Lima Basadre brought out the first volume of his *Historia del derecho Peruano,* and in 1939 at Lima he published his excellent *Historia de la república, 1822-1899.*

A record of military events in Peru's history may be found in the two-volume *Historia militar del Perú* (Lima, 1931) by Carlos Dellepiane. In 1931 also appeared a challenging volume by the statesman, diplomat, and internationalist Victor Andrés Belaunde (b.1883) entitled *La realidad nacional* (Paris, 1931). The author is well known for his writings in the field of diplomatic history.

A work of great value to historical scholars is the *Apéndice al diccionario histórico-biográfico del Perú,* compiled by Evaristo San Cristóval (b.1894) as a supplement to Mendiburu's great work already noted. Volume I appeared at Lima in 1935.

Two valuable textbooks written in this century by the widely known Carlos Wiesse (b.1859) are entitled *Las civilizaciones primitivas del Perú* (Lima, 1913) and *Historia del Perú colonial* (Lima, 1918). Other volumes by the same author are *Historia del Perú y de la civilización peruana* (Lima, 1917), *Historia del Perú independiente* (Lima, 1925), and *Historia del Perú* (4 vols., Lima, 1925-28).

Three recent volumes in Spanish dealing with the Inca civilization are *El imperio incaico* (Lima, 1931) by Horacio Urteaga (b.1887), *L'empire socialiste des Inka* (Paris, 1928) by Louis Baudin, and the *Pre-historia peruana* by Atilio Sivirichi (Lima, 1930).

English works which should be added to this list are C. R. Enock's *Peru,* published at London in 1908; Marie Wright's (b.1866) *The old and new Peru* (Philadelphia, 1908); Graham Henry Stuart's (b.1887) *The governmental system of Peru* (Washington, D.C., 1925); and Philip Ainsworth Means' *Fall of the Inca empire* (New York, 1932).

Among the recent volumes dealing with Peru are *Vida intelectual del virreinato del Perú* (Buenos Aires, 1937) by Felipe Barreda Laos (b.1888), the author of *Vida intelectual de la colonia* (Lima, 1909); *Historia república del Perú* from 1821 to 1933 (Lima, ca.1933) by Luis Humberto Delgado (b.1899), the author of *Historia de los gobiernos del Perú y de las presidentes de las Cámeras legislatives, 1821-1927,* the first volume of which was printed at Lima in 1927; *El virreinato del Peru . . .* (Lima, 1939), a critical study by José M. Valega; *Historia del Perú, descubrimiento, conquista, colonia . . .* (Lima, 1939), a textbook for *colegios* by Ricardo Mariátegui Oliva; and *Historia del Perú* (Lima, 1939), a book for college use by Rubén Vargas Ugarte.

18. Bolivia

There have been a number of valuable histories of Bolivia written in this century. In 1905 Daniel Sánchez Bustamante (b.1871) published at La Paz his volume of miscellaneous essays on various subjects dealing with the history and civilization of Bolivia and entitled *Opiniones y discursos.*

In 1912 appeared at La Paz the *Bosquejo de la historia de Bolivia* by Manuel Ordóñez López. In 1917 appeared at Madrid *La creación de Bolivia* by Sabino Pinilla (1851-1907), which was left uncompleted by the author's death and which carried the story to the year 1828. Two years later, in 1919, the two-volume *Historia general del Alto Perú* by Luis Pez was published at Sucre.

Between 1920 and 1924 at La Paz, Alcides Argüedas (b.1879), the foremost historian of Bolivia, published his four-volume *Historia de Bolivia,* which dealt with the foundation of the republic to about 1864. His one-volume *Historia general de Bolivia,* treating the period since 1809, was published at the same place in 1922 and appeared in French at Paris in 1932. In 1921 at Madrid appeared his *La fundación de la república.*

In 1925 at La Paz was published the first volume of a series entitled *Los primeros cien años de la república de Bolivia* by José Agustín Morales. This work includes many biographies of prominent Bolivians.

In 1935 Luis S. Crespo brought out at La Paz Volume I of his four-volume work entitled *Episodios históricos de Bolivia.*

A work in English by a French writer on economic subjects is entitled *Bolivia, its people and its resources* and was published at London and New York in 1914. The author, Paul Walle (b.1872), wrote many economic treatises dealing especially with Brazil.

Recent works on Bolivia are *Historia de la conquista del Oriente boliviano* (Buenos Aires, 1939) by Enrique Finot (b.1890); *Cuadro geográfico de la república de Bolivia* (La Paz, 1939), by Rómulo Ramírez O.; and *The political organization of Bolivia* (Washington, D.C., 1940) by N. A. N. Cleven.

19. Paraguay

Paraguay has received frequent treatment at the hands of historians. In 1902 José Segundo Decoud (1848-1909) published his *History of Paraguay* through the medium of the Government Printing Office at Washington, D.C. In 1906 at Asunción, Cecilio Báez (1862-1941) published his *Cuadros históricos y descriptivos.* In 1910 his *Resumen de la historia de Paraguay* was published at Asunción, and in 1926 his *Historia colonial del Paraguay* appeared at Asunción. The next year at Paris was published his *Le Paraguay,* which dealt with the evolution and general conditions of the country. During 1931 and 1932 appeared his *Historia diplomática del Paraguay* (2 vols., Asunción).

In 1911 appeared at Asunción Volume I of the *Estudio sobre la independencia del Paraguay* by Fulgencio R. Moreno (b.1872).

In 1912 at London W. H. Koebel brought out his book entitled *In Jesuit land,* which gave an account of the Jesuit missions, and in 1916 at London he published his *Paraguay.*

Three important works on the Paraguayan War should be mentioned. The first, in seven volumes (Buenos Aires, 1921-32), is entitled *La guerra del Paraguay.* The account is a military one, but it is carried only through 1866. The author is Juan Beverina. In 1929 appeared in two scholarly volumes *The origins of the Paraguayan war* by Pelham H. Box (1898-1937) at Urbana, Ill., of which a Spanish translation was published at Asunción in 1936; and in the same year (1929) Enrique de Gandía (b.1906) published his *Historia del Gran Chaco* at Buenos Aires.

The international relations of Paraguay have been comprehensively treated by Luis Alberto de Herrera (b.1873). From 1908 to 1926 appeared at Montevideo his five-volume *La diplomacia oriental en el Paraguay,* which chiefly concerns relations with Argentina and Uruguay. This had been preceded by his *La revolución francesa y Sud América* (Paris, 1905). Another volume by the same author is entitled *El Uruguay internacional* (Paris, 1912).

20. Argentina

Of the works concerning Argentina the following should be mentioned. In 1902 and 1903 appeared at Madrid in two volumes the *Historia de la Argentina* by Juan García Al-Deguer (b.1855). In 1903 the *République argentine* by Georges Hersent was published at Paris, dealing with contemporary conditions and speculating upon the future. In 1907 the *Lecciones de historia argentina* by Vicente Gambón (b.1857) appeared in two volumes at Buenos Aires. In 1910 at London appeared W. A. Hirst's *Argentina.* Also in 1910 there was published at Buenos Aires the four-volume *Historia constitucional de la república argentina* by Luis Vicente Varela (b.1845). The next year (1911) appeared at Boston *Argentina and her people today* by Nevin Otto Winter.

In 1912 a history in French by Roberto Levillier (b.1881), an Argentine diplomat, was published at Paris under the title *Les origines argentines.* A Spanish edition appeared at the same time and place under the title *Orígenes argentinos: la formación de un gran pueblo. . . .* In the same year also an interesting work of a special nature was published at Barcelona under the title *Influencia del clero en la independencia argentina.* The author was Agustín Piaggio.

In 1913 at Buenos Aires Ricardo Levene (b.1885), the widely known historical scholar and later president of the University of La Plata, published under the title *Lecturas de historia argentina* a two-volume work on the revolution and the period immediately following. A sixteenth edition of this work appeared in 1938. In 1937 an English translation in one volume was made by W. S. Robertson and published at Chapel Hill under the title *A history of Argentina.* During 1920-21 his *Ensayo histórico sobre la revolución de mayo y Mariano Moreno* was published in two volumes at Buenos Aires. In 1927 and 1928 appeared at Buenos Aires a two-volume edition of his *Investigaciones acerca de la historia del virreinato del Plata,* first published in one volume in 1915 at Buenos Aires. In 1936 at Buenos Aires appeared the first of ten volumes in the *Historia de la nación argentina,* written by a number of co-operating historians under the editorship of Dr. Levene. The period to be covered is from the earliest time to 1862. Subsequent volumes have appeared regularly.

A writer of wide reputation, Ricardo Jaimes Freyre (1840-1910), wrote numerous works on Tucumán. Among these are *El Tucumán del siglo XVI* (Buenos Aires, 1914) and *Historia del descubrimiento de Tucumán* (Buenos Aires, 1916).

In 1917 appeared the first volume of the illustrated *Manual de historia de la civilización argentina,* edited by Rómulo D. Carbia (b.1885). Among several other valuable works is his *Historia de la historiografía argentina* (Buenos Aires, 1925) revised as *Historia crítica de la historiografía argentina* (La Plata, 1939). The next year at Buenos Aires he issued his *La crónica oficial de las indias occidentales* dealing with the historiography of Hispanic America in the sixteenth, seventeenth, and eighteenth centuries.

An extremely valuable work for those interested in the history of the evolution of Argentine culture is *La literatura argentina . . .* , by Ricardo Rojas (b.1882). This appeared in four volumes at Buenos Aires between 1917 and 1922, and in eight volumes at Buenos Aires (1924-25) as Volumes VIII to XV of his *Obras.*

In 1918 José Ingenieros (1877-1925) brought out at Buenos Aires his extremely important two-volume work entitled *La evolución de las ideas argentinas.* In the same year Ismael Bucich Escobar published the first edition in one volume of his *Historia de los presidentes argentinos* (Buenos Aires, 1918). Subsequent editions contained two volumes. The latest edition appeared at Buenos Aires in 1934.

In 1920 Julio Cobos Daract (b.1883) published at Buenos Aires his two-volume *Historia argentina* which covers the Republican period. The next year at Buenos Aires appeared the *Nuevo diccionario geográfico histórico de la argentina* by Javier Marrazza, which constitutes a usable handbook. In 1921 and 1922 the *Historia argentina y americana* by Julián Rivera Campos was published in two volumes at Buenos Aires.

In 1925, probably at Buenos Aires, the Argentine sociologist, jurisconsult, and historian, Ernesto Quesada (1858-1934), published his chief historical work entitled *El ciclo cultural de la colonia.* This had been preceded and was followed by other works of a biographical, diplomatic, and philosophical nature.

In 1926 the *Historia de la república argentina* by Emilio Vera y González appeared at Buenos Aires in three volumes, beginning the story of the country in 1817 and carrying it to the date of publication. In the same year (1926) Emilio Ravignani (b.1886) published in three volumes at Buenos Aires his important study entitled *Historia constitucional de la república argentina.* A second revised edition was published at the same place in 1930. In 1926 also Roberto Levillier published the first volume of a series which he edited and which was entitled *Nueva crónica de la conquista del Tucumán* (Madrid and Buenos Aires) which concerns Argentine history from 1535 to 1617. The second volume was published at Warsaw in 1930, and a third volume appeared at the same place the next year. Many other valuable works have come from this author's scholarly pen, including *Organización de la iglesia y ordenes religiosas en el virreinato del Perú en el siglo XVI* (Madrid, 1919), *Los Incas del Perú* (Madrid, 1935), and others.

The economic historian will find an indispensable work in Alejandro E. Bunge's (b.1880) *La economía argentina,* published in four volumes at Buenos Aires in 1928 and 1929. In the latter year at Buenos Aires appeared the two-volume *Virtuas históricas* by Francisco Centeno (b.1862), which contained much material on the period between 1810 and 1928.

In 1931 Enrique de Gandía at Buenos Aires brought out his specialized *La historia de la conquista del Río de la Plata y del Paraguay . . . 1535-1556.* In the same year and in the same place appeared the monumental and much-needed four-volume work by José Pacífico Otero (1874-1937) entitled *Historia del libertador Don José de San Martín.*

A work dealing with religious affairs in the colony is entitled *Introducción a la historia eclesiástica del Tucumán* by the ethnologist, churchman, and historian Monseñor Pablo Cabrera (b.1857). It was published in two volumes at Buenos Aires in 1935 and is somewhat pro-Catholic in attitude.

Another recent work of a special nature is *La Patagonia y sus problemas* by Colonel José María Sarobe which appeared at Buenos Aires in 1935. This is an excellent, comprehensive, and much-needed survey of the region. Among other recent works of importance concerning Argentina are *Historia de la constitución argentina* (2 vols., Buenos Aires, 1935) by J. B. Lafonte; *Historia de la medicina argentina* (Buenos Aires, 1937) by José Luis Molinari; *Historia argentina. Política y militar de la civilización argentina* (Buenos Aires, 1937) by Vicente Passarelli; *Lecturas de historia argentina. Relatos de contemporáneos, 1527-1870* (Buenos Aires, 1938) by José Luis Busaniche; *Conquistadores del Río de la Plata* (Buenos Aires, 1937) by Ricardo de Lafuente Machaín (b.1882); *El arte de los Argentinos* (3 vols., Buenos Aires, 1937-40) by José León Pagano (b.1875); *Historia de la ciudad de Buenos Aires* (Buenos Aires, Vol. I, 1936; Vol. II, 1937) by the prolific Argentine scholar Enrique de Gandía and Alfonso Rómulo Zabala (b.1884); *Las invasiones inglesas del Río de la Plata, 1806-1807* (Buenos Aires, 1936) by Carlos Roberts; and *Lecciones de historia argentina* (Buenos Aires, 1940), a text for college classes, by Eulalio Astudillo Menéndez (b.1886).

The chief English writer who dealt with Argentina in this century was W. H. Koebel, who published several books in rapid succession. In 1907 he brought out his *Modern Argentina* at London. This was followed by his *L'Argentine moderne* (Paris, 1909); his *Argentina past and present* (London, 1910); his *Romance of the River Plate* (2 vols., London, 1914); his *Great southland* (London, 1919); and *The new Argentina* (London and New York, 1923).

A valuable specialized treatment on Argentina is entitled *The federal system of the Argentine Republic* by Leo S. Rowe (b.1871) and was published by the Carnegie Institution of Washington in 1921 as one of a series of studies on Hispanic American political and constitutional development.

Another work in English is the *Argentine Republic* (London, 1922) by Pierre Denis, while the most recent volume is entitled *A history of the Argentine Republic* (Cambridge, England, 1931) by Frederick Alexander Kirkpatrick (b.1861).

21. *Uruguay*

A leading history of Uruguay in this century is by Pablo Blanco Acevedo and it was published in six volumes at Montevideo between 1901 and 1913 under the title *Historia del Uruguay*. Another valuable work for the historian of the country is the *Diccionario popular de historia de la república O. del Uruguay* by the exceedingly productive scholar Orestes Araújo (b.1853), published in three volumes at Montevideo between 1901 and 1903. In this latter year and the next at Montevideo appeared the second edition of the same author's two-volume *Gobernantes del Uruguay*. This was followed in 1907 by his *Historia compendio de la civilización uruguaya*, printed at Montevideo in two volumes. Three years later appeared his *Nueva historia del Uruguay* in two volumes at the same place.

In the latter year (1910) Juan Zorrilla de San Martín (b.1855) brought out at Montevideo his two-volume *La epopeya de Artigas*, which dealt with the contemporary epoch of that hero. The next year W. H. Koebel published at London and New York his survey of the country under the title *Uruguay*.

In 1916 was published at Montevideo the first volume of the *Manual de historia de Uruguay* by Eduardo Acevedo (b.1858). This had been preceded in 1908 at the same place by his two-volume *Notas y apuntes*, which dealt with the economic and financial problems of the republic. His greatest work bears the title *Anales históricos del Uruguay*, published at Montevideo in six volumes between 1933 and 1936. It is the best and most comprehensive history of the country.

In 1919 appeared at Montevideo the valuable *Historia de la dominación portuguesa en el Uruguay*, covering the years from 1810 to 1830. The author was Mario Falcao Espalter (b.1892).

A work of great special value to the historian of Uruguayan colonial and modern life appeared in three volumes at Montevideo in 1930 under the title *Proceso intelectual del Uruguay y crítica de su literatura*. The author was Alberto Zum Felde (b.1888), who is remembered for his valuable sociological and historical essay, *Proceso histórico del Uruguay* (Montevideo, 1919).

In 1930 also appeared at Montevideo the first volume of the *Historia de la república oriental del Uruguay* by José Salgado (b.1875), while the next year at the same place was published the two-volume *El Uruguay entre dos siglos (apuntes para un programa de la nueva etapa)* by Manuel Bernárdez (b.1868).

A recent volume dealing with the period since 1810 is by Pedro Riva-Zucchelli and is entitled *Historia de la independencia de la República Oriental del Uruguay.* It was published at Montevideo in 1934.

In 1936 at Montevideo was published Volume I of *La independencia de la banda oriental,* the work of the political scientist, historian, and biographer Setembrino Ezekial Pereda (b.1859). This author has produced a number of important studies for the historian, among them being *Garibaldi en el Uruguay* (3 vols., Montevideo, 1914-16) and *El poder ejecutivo* (4 vols., Montevideo, 1918-23).

A valuable volume for the economic historian of Uruguay covering the period from 1934 to 1937 is *Utopia in Uruguay* (New York, 1938) by Simon G. Hanson.

22. *Chile*

Among the productive scholars of twentieth-century Chile is Domingo Amunátegui Solar (b.1860). From 1901 to 1904 he published at Santiago, Chile, his *La sociedad chilena del siglo XVIII* in three volumes. In 1909 and 1910 appeared at Santiago his two-volume *Las encomiendas de indíjenas en Chile.* In 1915 he brought out his *Bosquejo histórico de la literatura chilena* at Santiago. In 1923 appeared at the same place his two-volume *Bajo la dominación española* covering Chilean history to 1808. In 1925 he published at Santiago his *Historia de Chile* in one volume and in 1930 appeared *Los próceres de la independencia de Chile* (Santiago) and the *Nacimiento de la república de Chile* (Santiago) dealing with the period from 1803 to 1833. In 1932 appeared the first volume of his *Historia social de Chile* at Santiago. In 1937 was published at Santiago his *La sociedad de Santiago en el siglo XVII.*

In 1901 and 1902 at Santiago José Toribio Medina published his two-volume *Relaciones de Chile,* based upon early chronicles of the Indies. Up to the time of his death in 1930 this prolific and scholarly historian continued to publish many valuable works, including histories of printing, biographies, bibliographies, and works of a more general nature.

At Santiago in 1903 Alejandro Fuenzalida Grandón (b.1865) brought out his *Historia del desarrollo intelectual de Chile (1541-1810).* In 1906 at the same place he published *La evolución social de Chile (1541-1810).* Both of these works contain valuable material for the historian.

In 1903 Alberto Edwards (1874-1932) published his *Bosquejo histórico de los partidos políticos chilenos* at Santiago. Two of his more recent important works are *La fronda aristocrática en Chile* (Santiago, 1927) and *El gobierno de Don Manuel Montt, 1851-1861* (Santiago, 1932).

In 1905 and 1906 *Un decenio de la historia de Chile (1841-1851)* by Diego Barros Arana was published at Santiago. In 1906 and 1907 Louis Galdames published at Santiago his illustrated two-volume *Estudio de la historia de Chile* (later printed in one volume) and in 1925 the first volume of his *Historia de Chile, la evolución constitucional.*

In 1908 the *Historia de Chile durante los gobiernos de García Ramón, Merlo de la Fuente y Jaraquemada* was published in two volumes at Santiago by Crescente Errázuriz (1849-1931), the archbishop of Santiago. This was a continuation of his *Seis años de la historia de Chile,* which had been published in two volumes at Santiago in 1881. Between 1908 and 1913 there appeared at Santiago the three-volume *Los conquistadores de Chile,* which was the work of Tomás Thayer Ojeda (b.1877).

In 1910 Benjamín Vicuña Subercaseaux (b.1876) published his *Crónicas del centenaria: la colonia—la patria vieja* at Santiago, which traced Chilean history to 1821, and during 1911 and 1912 his two-volume *Historia de Chile,* which dealt with Chilean history to 1810.

In 1911 the famed internationalist Alejandro Álvarez (b.1868) published at Santiago his *Rasgos generales de la historia diplomática de Chile, 1810-1910,* and in 1916 at the same place his *Diplomacia de Chile* covering the years 1810 to 1824.

Between 1912 and 1919 at Valparaiso appeared the three-volume *Guerra del Pacífico* by the widely known Gonzalo Bulnes, the first volume of which appeared at the time in a third edition. The title of this work is somewhat misleading, since the treatment covers the years 1829 to 1887. Meanwhile, in 1914 at Santiago was printed the posthumous *La revolución de 1891,* the work of Fanor Velasco (ca.1843-1907).

In 1924 there was published at Madrid the public school textbook by Indalecio Téllez under the title *Historia de Chile.* The next year at Santiago appeared the *Historia eclesiástica de Chile* by Bishop Carlos Silva Cotapos, which dealt with the activities of the Catholic Church and its clergy. Between 1925 and 1927 at Santiago was printed the two-volume *Historia de Chile* by Tomás Guevara Silva (b.1865), covering only the prehistoric civilizations.

A history of Chile by a literary man is entitled *Histoire du Chili.* Published at Paris in 1927 and dealing with history and literary criticism, its author was Leonardo Peña.

Among the most widely known contemporary historians of Chile was Agustín Edwards (1878-1941). In 1929 at London appeared the first of six volumes dealing with Chilean life and history. It is entitled *Peoples of old* and treats the colonial period. The second volume was published at

London in 1931 under the title *The Dawn* and at Valparaiso the same year with the title *El alba.* This work deals with the birth and consolidation of Chile in the decades immediately following 1810.

Several English works dealing with Chile should be mentioned, the chief of which are *The republic of Chile* (Philadelphia, 1904) by Marie Robinson Wright; *Chile, its history and development* (New York, 1907) by G. P. Scott-Elliott; *Chile and her people today* (Boston, 1912) by N. O. Winter; *Modern Chile* (London, 1913) by W. H. Koebel; *Chile, its land and people* (London, 1914) by Francis J. G. Maitland; and *Chile: land and society* (New York, 1936) by George McCutchen McBride.

Among recent works in Spanish dealing with Chile which will be found of value to the student of history are *Historia general* (3 vols., Santiago, 1933-37) by Francisco Frias Valenzuela; *Geografía de Chile* (Santiago, 1938) by Vicente Bustos Pérez, who in 1939 brought out the twenty-first edition of his brief *Historia de Chile* (Santiago); *El cabildo en Chile colonial* (Santiago, 1940) by Julio Alemparte R.; and *Historia de Chile desde la prehistoria hasta 1891* (volume I, Santiago, 1940?) by Francisco Antonio Encina (b.1874).

A SELECTED LIST OF BIBLIOGRAPHICAL AND BIOGRAPHICAL COLLECTIONS AND AIDS

For further information concerning histories and historians of Hispanic America, the student is directed to the following sources of bio-bibliographical data not previously cited:

Acevedo Escobedo, Antonio (b. 1909), *Guía bibliográfica de la historia de México* (Mexico, 1935).

Aita, Antonio (b. 1891), *La literatura argentina contemporanea* (Buenos Aires, 1931).

Alcover y Beltrán, Antonio Miguel (1875-1915), *Los libros de producción latino-americano* (Habana, 1912).

Alonso Cortés, Narciso (b.1875), *Historia de la literatura española* (Valladalad, 4th ed., 1940?).

Altamira, Rafael (b. 1866), and José María Ots Capdequí, *Bibliographie des études sur l'histoire coloniale provenant d'auteurs espagnols ou publiés en Espagne, 1900-1931* (Paris, 1932).

Andrade, José María, *Catalogue de la riche bibliothèque de D. José María Andrade* (Paris, 1869).

Andrade, Vicente de Paulo (1844-1915), *Ensayo bibliográfico mexicano del siglo XVII* (2 volumes, Mexico, 1899-1909).

Annaes de bibliotheca nacional do Rio de Janeiro (50 volumes, Rio de Janeiro, 1876-1936).

Anrique Reyes, Nicolás (d. 1904), *Bibliografía marítima chilena, 1840-1894* (Santiago, Chile, 1894).

——, *Ensayo de una bibliografía jeográfica de Chile* (Santiago, Chile, 1902).

Antonio, Nicolás (1617-1684), *Bibliotheca hispana nova* (2 volumes, Rome, 1672).

Anuario bibliográfico mexicano (Mexico, 1931 ff).

Arango Ferrer, Javier, *La literatura de Colombia* (Buenos Aires, 1940).

Arboleda R., Gustavo (b. 1881), *Diccionario biográfico del Ecuador* (Quito, 1910).

Arias, Augusto, *Panorama de la litertura ecuatoriana* (Quito, 1936).

Arrieta, Rafael Alberto, *Don Gregorio Beéche y los bibliógrafos Americanistas de Chile y del Plata* (La Plata, 1941).

Asher, Adolph [originally Abraham] (1800-1853), *A short bibliographical memoir* (Frankfurt and Nuremberg, 1833).

——, *Bibliographical essay . . .* (Berlin. 1839).

Asher, Georg Michael (d. 1905), *A bibliographical and historical essay on the Dutch books and pamphlets relating to . . . its possessions in Brazil* (2 parts, Amsterdam, 1854-1867).

Atkinson, Geoffray (b. 1892), *La littérature geographique française* (Paris, 1927).

Avellaneda, Nicolás, *Grandes escritores argentinos* (Buenos Aires, 1927).

Bachiller y Morales, Antonio (1812-1889), *Apuntes para la historia de las letras de la isla de Cuba* (Habana, 1861).

Backer, Augustin de (1809-1873), Aloys de Backer (1823-1883), and Carlos Sommervogel (1834-1902), *Bibliothèque des écrivains de la Compagnie de Jésus . . .* (10 volumes, Paris and Brussels, 1890-1909), and a supplement in 5 parts (Toulouse, 1911-1930) by Ernest-M. Rivière (b. 1854).

Baginsky, Paul Ben, *German works relating to America, 1493-1800* (New York, 1942).

Ballester, Rafael, *Bibliografía de la historia de España. Catálogo metódico y cronológico de las fuentas y obras principales relativas a la historia de España desde los orígenes hasta nuestros días* (Vol. I, Gerona, 1921).

Barbosa Machado, Diego (1682-1772), *Bibliotheca lusitana histórica, crítica e cronológica* (4 volumes, Lisbon, 1741-1759).

Barcia Carballido y Zúñiga, Andrés González, *Historiadores primitivos de las indias occidentales* (3 volumes, Madrid, 1749).

Barrera, Isaac J. (b. 1884), *Historia de la literatura hispanoamericana* (Quito, 1934).

——, *Literatura ecuatoriana* (Quito, 1926).

Barringer, Georges A., *Catologue de l'histoire de l'Amérique* (5 volumes, Paris, 1903-11).

Barros Arana, Diego (1830-1907), *Notas para una bibliografía de obras anóminas i seudónimas sobre la historia, la jeografía i la literatura de América* (Santiago, Chile, 1882).

Bartlett, John Russell (1805-1886), *Bibliographical notices of rare and curious books relating to America in the library of the late John Carter Brown* (2 volumes, Providence, 1875-82).

Batres Jáuregui, Antonio (b. 1847), *Bibliográfía histórico guatemalteca* (Guatemala, 1908).

Beers, Henry Putney (b. 1907), *Bibliographies in American history* (New York, 1938, rev. ed., 1942).

Bell, Aubrey Fitzgerald (b. 1882), *Portuguese bibliography* (Oxford, 1922).

Beltrán, Oscar R. (b.1896), *Manual de la literatura hispanoamericana* (Buenos Aires, 1938).

Bemis, Samuel Flagg (b. 1891), and Grace Gardner Griffin, *Guide to the diplomatic history of the United States, 1775-1921* (Washington, 1935).

Beristain de Sousa, José Mariano (1756-1817), *Biblioteca hispanoamericana septentrional* (3 volumes, Santiago, Chile, 1816-21).

Bezerra, Alcides, *Bibliographia historica do primeiro reinado a maioridade 1822-1840* (Rio de Janeiro, 1936).

Bibliografía española (Madrid, 1901-22).

Bibliografía general española e hispanoamericana, volumes for 1923, 1925, 1927, and 1929 (Madrid, 1925-30).

"Bibliografía hispanoamericana" in *Revista Hispánica Moderna* (New York, October 1934 ff.).

Biblioteca de autores españoles (71 volumes, Madrid, 1850-82).

Bibliotheca Americana . . . offered for sale by John Russell Smith (1810-1894), (London, 1865).

Bibliotheca Nacional, *Catalogo de exposição da historia do Brasil* (2 volumes, Rio de Janeiro, 1891).

Biografías de literatos nacionales (Guatemala, 1889).

Biolley, Pablo, "Bibliografía . . ." in *Revista de Costa Rica en el Siglo XIX* (Vol. I, San José, 1902).

Blake, A. V. A. do Sacremento (b. 1827), *Diccionario bibliografico brasileiro* (7 volumes, Rio de Janeiro, 1883-1902).

Blake, W. W. (1850-1918), *Ninth catalogue of second-hand books . . . relating chiefly to Spanish America* (Mexico, 1910).

Borchard, E. M. (b. 1884), *Guide to the law and legal literature of Argentina, Brazil, and Chile,* (Washington, 1917).

Brasseur de Bourbourg, Charles-Étienne (1814-1874). *Bibliothèque mexico-guatémalienne . . .* (Paris, 1871).

Briseño, Ramón (b. 1814), *Estadística bibliográfica de la literatura chilena* (2 volumes, Santiago, Chile, 1862-79).

Brunet, Jacques-Charles (1780-1867), *Manuel de libraire* (6 volumes, Paris, 1860-1880).

Burger, Konrad (1856-1912), *Die drucker und verleger in Spanien und Portugal von 1501-1536* (Leipzig, 1913).

Butler, Ruth Lapham (b. 1896), *A check list of manuscripts in the Edward E. Ayer collection* (Chicago, 1937).

Calcagno, Francisco (b.1829), *Diccionario biográfico cubano [hasta 1878]* (New York, 1878; Havana, 1885-86).

Camus, Armond Gaston (1740-1804), *Memoires sur la collection des grandes et petits voyages . . .* (Paris, 1802).

Carayon, Auguste (1813-1874), *Bibliographie historique de la Compagnie de Jésus* (Paris, 1864).

Carvalho, Alfredo de (b. 1854), *Bibliotheca exotica-bresileira* (Rio de Janeiro, 1929).

Carvalho, Ronald de (1893-1935), *Pequena historia da literatura brasileira* (Rio de Janeiro, 6th ed., 1937).

Catálogo general de la libreria española e hispanoamericana, años 1901-1930 (Madrid and Barcelona, 1932 ff.).

Catálogo razonado, primera parte, Biblioteca Enrique Arana (Buenos Aires, 1935).

Catalogue of the Spanish library and of the Portuguese books bequeathed by George Ticknor to the Boston Public Library . . . by James Lyman Whitney (Boston 1879).

Chadenat, Charles, *Bibliotheca braziliensis* (Paris, n.d.).

Chiappa, Victor M., *Noticias biográficas sobre la Colección de historiadores de Chile . . .* (Santiago, 1905).

Church, E. D. (1835-1910). *A catalogue of books relating to the discovery and early history of North and South America* (5 volumes, New York, 1907-1909).
Clements, William L., *The William L. Clements Library of Americana at the University of Michigan* (Ann Arbor, 1923).
Coester, Alfred Lester (b. 1874), "A bibliography of Spanish-American literature" in *Romantic Review,* III (January-March, 1912), p. 68-101.
Consiglieri Pedroso, Zophimo, *Catalogo bibliographico des publicacões relativas aos descobrimentos portugueses* (Lisbon, 1912).
Cotarelo y Mori, Emilio (1857-1936), *Diccionario biográfico y bibliográfico de calígrafos españoles* (2 volumes, Madrid, 1913-16).
Coulter, Edith, and Melanie Gerstenfeld, *Historical bibliographies. A systematic and annotated guide* (Berkeley, 1935).
Cowan, R. E. (b. 1862), and R. G., *Bibliography of the history of California, 1510-1930* (3 volumes, San Francisco, 1933).
Cox, Edward Godfrey, *A reference guide to the literature of travel . . .* Volume II, *The New World* (Seattle, 1938).
Cruz, Manuel de la (1861-1896), *Literatura cubana* (Madrid, 1924).
Cruz, Pedro Nolasco (1859-1939), *Estudios sobre la literatura chilena* (3 volumes, Santiago, 1926-40).
Cundall, F. (1858-1937), *Bibliography of the West Indies* (Kingston, 1909).

Dalrymple, Alexander (1737-1808), *Catalogue of authors who have written on Río de la Plata, Paraguay, and Chaco* (London, 1807).
Darnet de Ferreyra, Ana Julia, *Historia de la literatura española y argentina* (Buenos Aires, new ed., 1940).
Decoud, John M. (1848-1909), *A list of books, magazine articles, and maps relating to Paraguay* (Washington, 1904).
Desdevises du Dezert, Georges Nicolas (b. 1854), "Les sources manuscrites de l'histoire de l'Amérique Latine à la fin du XVIIIe siecle (1760-1807)" in *Nouvelles archives des missions scientifiques et littéraires* (Nouv. ser., XII, 1914).
Diccionario biográfico de Chile, 1936 (Santiago, Chile).
Diccionario enciclopédico hispano-americano de literatura, ciencias y artes (23 volumes in 24, Barcelona, 1887-98; 2 volumes apéndice, 1898-99; 3 volumes apéndice segundo, 1907-1910).
Dobles Segrada, Luis, *Indice bibliográfico de Costa Rica* (9 volumes, San José, 1927-36).
Dorsey, George Amos (1868-1931), *A bibliography of the anthropology of Peru* (Chicago, 1898).
Durón y Gamero, Rómulo Enrique (b. 1865), *Honduras literaria* (2 volumes, Tegucigalpa, 1896).

Economic literature of Latin America (2 volumes, Cambridge, Mass., 1935-36).
Eguiara y Eguren, Juan José de (d. 1763), *Bibliotheca mexicana* (Mexico, 1755).

Elías de Molins, Antonio (1850-1909), *Ensayo de una bibliografía literaria de España y América* (2 volumes, Madrid, 1902).

Encina, Francisco Antonio (b. 1874), *La literatura histórica chilena* (Santiago, 1935).

Erazo, Salvador L., *Internacionalistas latino-americanas* (San Salvador, 1910).

Espasa, José (ed.), *Enciclopedia universal ilustrada europea-americana* (70 volumes, Madrid and Barcelona, 1912-30). Also *Apéndice* (10 volumes, Madrid and Barcelona, 1930-33) and *Suplemento anual* (Madrid and Barcelona, 1934-).

Esteves Pereira, João Manuel, *Portugal; diccionario historico, chorographico, heraldico, biographico, bibliographico* . . . (7 volumes, Lisbon, 1904-15).

Estrada, Genaro (1887-1937), *Monografías bibliográficas mexicanas* (Mexico, 1925 ff).

Estrella Gutiérrez, Fermín (b. 1900), *Historia de la literatura americana y argentina* (Buenos Aires, 2nd ed., 1941?)

Evans, Charles (b. 1850), *American bibliography. A chronological dictionary of all books, pamphlets, and periodical publications printed in the United States . . . 1639-1920.* (12 volumes, Chicago, 1903-1934).

Faribault, George Barthelemy (1789-1866), *Catalogue d'ouvrages sur l'histoire de l'Amérique* . . . (Quebec, 1837).

Feliú Cruz, Guillermo (b. 1901), *Bibliografía de Don José Toribio Medina* (Buenos Aires, 1931).

——, *Ensayo de una bibliografía de la obras de Don Benjamín Vicuña Mackenna* (Santiago, 1932).

Fernández de Castillo, Francisco (b. 1864), *Libros y libreros en el siglo XVI* (Mexico, 1914).

Ferreira, Joaquim, *Historia da literatura portuguesa* (O Porto, 1939).

Field, T. W. (1820-1881), *An essay towards an Indian bibliography* (New York, 1873).

Figanière, Jorge César de (1813-1888), *Bibliographia historica portugueza* (Lisbon, 1850).

Figueroa, Pedro Pablo (1857-1909), *Diccionario biográfico de Chile* (3 volumes, Santiago, 1897-1901).

Figueroa, Virgilio (b. 1870), *Diccionario histórico, biográfico y bibliográfico de Chile* (5 volumes in 4, Santiago, 1925-1931).

Ford, J. D. M. (b. 1873) (general editor), *Bibliographies of the belles-lettres of Latin America* (19 volumes, Cambridge, Mass., 1931-1935).

Foulché-Delbosc, Raymond (1864-1929), *Bibliographie des voyages en Espagne et en Portugal* (Paris, 1896).

Franulic, Lenka, *Cien autores contemporáneos* (2 volumes, Santiago, Chile, 2nd ed., 1941).

Fumagalli, Giuseppe (b. 1863), and Pietro Amat di S. Filippo (1826-1895), "Bibliografia Italo-Americana della geografia di America" in *Commissione Colombiana. Raccolta di documenti e studi* (Rome, 1892-93, Part VI, p. 113-217).

Gallardo, Bartolomé José (1776-1852), *Ensayo de una biblioteca española de libros raros y curiosos* (4 volumes, Madrid, 1863-89).

García, Perfecto (booksellers), *Bibliografía americana, especialidad en obras de autores argentinos . . . desde 1796 hasta 1853* (Buenos Aires, 1916).

García, Rodolpho, "Bibliographia geographica brasileira" in *Revisto do Instituto Historico y Geographico Brasileiro* (Rio de Janeiro, 1919, Vol. LXXXV, p. 5-100).

García Calderón, V. (b. 1886), *Biblioteca de cultura peruana* (12 volumes in 3, Paris, 1938).

García Carraffa, Alberto (b. 1882), and Arturo (b. 1876), *Enciclopedia heráldica y genealógica hispano-americana* (59 volumes, Madrid, 1920-36).

García Godoy, Federico (1857-1924), *La literatura americana de nuestros días* (Madrid, 1934).

García Icazbalceta, Joaquín (1825-1894), *Bibliografía mexicana del siglo XVI* (Madrid, 1886).

——, *Catálogo de la colección de manuscritos relativos a la historia de América* (Mexico, 1927).

García Rico y Cía, *Biblioteca hispánica* (Madrid, 1916), and *Suplemento primero* (Madrid, 1920).

García Velloso, Enrique (b. 1880), *Historia de la literatura argentina* (Buenos Aires, 1914).

Garnett, Richard (1835-1906), "Paraguayan and Argentine bibliography" in *Bibliographica* (London, 1895, Vol. I, p. 262-73).

Garraux, A. L. (b. 1833), *Bibliographie brésilienne. Catologue des ouvrages français et latins relatifs au Brésil, 1500-1898* (Paris, 1898).

Gayangos y Arce, Pascual de (1809-1897), *Catologue of the manuscripts in the Spanish language in the British Museum* (4 volumes, London, 1875-93).

Geigel y Zenón, José (1841-1892), and Abelardo Morales Ferrer, *Bibliografía puertorriqueña. Escrita en 1492-1894* (Barcelona, 1934).

Geiger, Maynard, *A biographical dictionary of Franciscans in Spanish Florida and Cuba* (Paterson, N.J., 1940).

——, "The Franciscan historian and history writing" in the Franciscan Educational Conference, *Report of the Eighteenth Annual Meeting,* Vol. XVIII, no. 18 (December, 1936), p. 359-74.

Giorgi, Manuel V., *Curso de historia de la literatura hispanoamericana* (Buenos Aires, 1937).

Goldsmith, Peter H. (1865-1926), *A brief bibliography of books in English, Spanish, and Portuguese relating to the republics commonly called Latin America* (New York, 1915).

González, Silvino M., and Nestor Herrera Gómez, *Apuntes para una bibliografía militar de México, 1536-1936* (Mexico, 1936).

González Peña, Carlos (b. 1885), *Historia de la literatura mexicana* (Mexico, 2nd ed., 1940).

González Suárez, Federico (1844-1917), *Bibliografía ecuatoriana . . . 1750-1792* (Quito, 1892).

Grässe, Johann Georg Theodor (1814-1855), *Trésor de livres rares et précieux* (7 volumes, Paris, 1859-69).

Griffin, Grace Gardiner, *Writings in American history* (Washington, 1906 ff).

Grismer, Raymond L., *A bibliography of articles and essays on the literature of Spain and Spanish America* (Minneapolis, 1935).

——, *A reference index to twelve thousand Spanish American authors* (New York, 1939).

—— and J. E. Lepine, and R. H. Olmstead, *A bibliography of articles on Spanish literature* (Minneapolis, 1933).

Gubernatis, Angelo de (1840-1913), *Dictionnaire international des écrivains du monde latin* (Rome, 1905).

Guia bibliográfica de la historia de México. Época precortesiana (Mexico, 1935).

Guzmán, Raz, and Jesús Guzmán, *Bibliografía de la independencia de México* (Mexico, Vols. I, II, 1938; Vol. III, 1939).

Haebler, Konrad (b. 1857), *Bibliografía ibéria del siglo XV* . . . (2 volumes, The Hague, 1903-17).

Haferkorn, Henry Ernest (b. 1859), *The war with Mexico, 1846-1848; a select bibliography* (Washington, 1914).

Handbook of Latin American studies . . . (6 volumes, Cambridge, 1936-41).

Harrisse, Henry (1830-1910), *Bibliotheca americana vetustissima* (2 volumes, Paris, 1866-1872).

Heber, Richard (1773-1833), *Bibliotheca heberiana* (13 volumes in 4, London, 1834-1837).

Heredia y Livermoore, Ricardo, *Catalogue de la bibliothèque* (4 volumes, Paris, 1891-94).

Hespelt, E. Herman, ed. *An outline history of Spanish American literature* (New York, 1941).

Hidalgo, Dionisio (1809-1866), *Diccionario general de bibliografía española* (7 volumes, Madrid, 1862-81).

Hispanic Society of America, *Bibliographie hispanique, 1905-1915* (11 volumes, New York, 1909-15).

——, *List of printed books in the library of the Hispanic Society of America* (20 volumes, New York, 1910).

Holmes, Ruth E. V. (b. 1901), *Bibliographical and historical description of the rarest books in the Oliveira Lima collection at the Catholic University of America* (Washington, 1926).

Homer, Arthur (1758-1806), *Bibliotheca americana* . . . (London, 1789).

Huneeus Gana, Jorge (b. 1866), *Biblioteca des escritores de Chile* . . . (Santiago, 1910).

Hunnewell, James Frothingham (1832-1910), *Illustrated Americana, 1493-1889* (n.p., 1890), edition limited to 150 copies.

Hurtado y Jiménez de la Serna, Juan (b. 1875), and Cándido Angel González Palencia (b. 1889), *Historia de la literatura española* (Madrid, 3rd ed., 1932).

Ibero-Amerikanisches Archiv (Berlin, 1931 ff.).

Iguiniz, J. B., *Bibliografía biográfica mexicana* (Vol. I, Mexico, 1930).

Ispizúa, Segundo de (1869-1924), *Bibliografía histórica sudamericana . . .* (Bilbao, 1915).

Jacob, Ernest Gerhard, "Literaturbericht aus der ibero-amerikanischen kulterwelt" in *Archiv f. Kulturgeschichte,* Vol. XXV, p. 231-50.

John Carter Brown Library, *Bibliotheca americana* (5 volumes, Providence, 1919-31).

Jones, C. K. (b. 1872), *Hispanic American bibliographies* (Baltimore, 1922), and *supplements* (1926 ff.).

——, *Latin American bibliographies* (Washington, 1942).

Kaiser, John Boynton (b. 1887), *The national bibliographies of the South American republics* (Boston, 1913).

Keniston, Ralph Hayward (b. 1883), *List of works for the study of Hispanic American history* (New York, 1920).

Kennett, White (1660-1728), *Bibliothecae americanae primordia* (London, 1713).

Knapp, William Ireland (1835-1909), *Biblioteca escogida de literatura española* (Madrid, 1875).

Larrabure y Unánue, Eugenio (1844-1916), *Les archives de indes et la bibliothèque Colombine de Séville . . .* (Paris, 1914).

Latassa y Ortín, Félix de (1733-1805), *Bibliotecas nueva de los escritores aragoneses . . . 1500 [hasta 1795]* (6 volumes, Pamphlona, 1798-1802).

——, *Bibliotecas antigua y nueva de escritores aragoneses* (3 volumes, Zaragossa, 1884-86).

Laval, Ramón A. (b. 1864), *Bibliografía de bibliografías chilenas* (Santiago, Chile, 1915).

——, *Biblioteca hispano-chilena, 1583-1817* (3 volumes, Santiago, Chile, 1898-99).

Laverde Amaya, Isodoro, *Bibliografía colombiana* (Bogotá, 1895).

Leclerc, Charles (1843-1889), *Bibliotheca americana* (Paris, 1867). A second catalogue was published in Paris in 1878, and two supplements were issued (Paris, 1881 and 1887).

Lehmann-Haupt, Hellmut (b. 1903), *Das Amerikanische buchwesen* (Leipzig, 1937).

Lenglet Dufresnoy, Nicolas (1674-1755), *Méthode pour étudier la géographie* (4 volumes, Paris, 1716). A fourth edition in ten volumes was published at Paris in 1768.

——, Méthode pour étudier l'histoire . . . (6 volumes Paris, 1729-40). A revised edition in fifteen volumes was published in Paris in 1772.

Lenhart, John M., "Franciscan histories of North America" in the Franciscan Educational Conference, *Report of the Eighteenth Annual Meeting*, Volume XVIII, no. 18 (December 1936) p. 1-52.

León, Nicolás (1859-1929), *Bibliografía mexicana del siglo XVIII* (5 volumes, Mexico, 1902-08).

León Pinelo, Antonio Rodríguez de (d. 1660), *Epítome de la biblioteca oriental y occidental, naútica y geográfica* (Madrid, 1629). First edition of the earliest bibliography relating to America.

Luquiens, F. B. (1876-1940), *Spanish American literature in the Yale University Library: a bibliography* (New Haven, 1939).

Macedo, Sergio D. T. de, *A literatura do Brasil colonial* (Rio de Janeiro, 1939?).

Maggs Brothers of London, *Bibliotheca americana* (7 parts, London, 1922-28).

Manchester, Alan K. (b. 1897), "Descriptive bibliography of the Brazilian section of the Duke University Library", in *Hispanic American Historical Review* (May and November, 1933).

——, "Some Brazilian colonial historians" in *Bulletin* of the Pan American Union (September and October, 1934).

Marinello, Juan (b. 1899), *Literatura hispanoamericana: hombres, meditaciones* (Mexico, 1937).

Martin, P. A. (1879-1942) *Who's who in Latin America* (Stanford University, 1935, 1940).

Matos-Hurtado, B., *Compendio de la historia de la literatura colombiana* (Bogotá, 1925).

Matulka, Barbara, "Recent Spanish American bibliographies" in *Romance Review* (New York, 1933, Vol. XXIV, p. 237-43).

Means, Philip Ainsworth (b. 1892), *Biblioteca andina* (Part I, New Haven, 1928).

Medina, José Toribio (1852-1930), *Biblioteca hispano-americana* (7 volumes, Santiago, Chile, 1898 1907).

——, *Biblioteca hispano-chilena* (3 volumes, Santiago, Chile, 1897-99).

Mejía de Fernández, Abigail, *Historia de la literatura dominicana* (Ciudad Trujillo, 1937).

Mencos Franco, Agustín (1882-1902) *Literatura guatemalteca en el período de la colonia* (Guatemala, 1937).

Méndez Bejarano, Mario (b. 1857), *Bio-bibliografía hispánica de Ultramar* . . . (Madrid, 1916).

Mensel, Johann Georg (1743-1820), *Bibliotheca historica* (Leipzig, 1782).

Merchand Pérez, B., *Diccionario biográfico del Ecuador* (Quito, 1928).

Meyer, Hermann Henry Bernard (1864-1937), *List of references on the Monroe Doctrine* (Washington, 1919).

Montt, Luis (1848-1909), *Bibliografía chilena* . . . (3 volumes, Santiago, Chile, 1904-21).

Morel-Fatio, Alfred Paul Victor (b. 1850), *Catalogue des manuscrits espagnols et portugais de la Bibliothèque Nationale* (Paris, 1892).

Moses, Bernard (1846-1930), *Spanish colonial literature in South America* (New York and London, 1922).
Motta, Arthur, *Historia da literatura brasileira* (2 volumes, São Paulo, 1930).
Muller, Frederik (1817-1881), *Catalogue of books, maps, plates on America and of a remarkable collection of early voyages* (Amsterdam, 1872).

Navarrete, Martín Fernández de (1765-1844), *Biblioteca marítima española* (2 volumes, Madrid, 1851).
New York Public Library, *List of works . . . relating to Mexico* (New York, 1909).
——, *List of works relating to the West Indies* (New York, 1912).
Nolasco Cruz, Pedro (b. 1859), *Estudios sobre la literatura chilena* (Santiago, Chile, 1926).

Obregón, Luis Gonzáles (1865-1938), *Cronistas e historiadores* (Mexico, 1936).
O'Halloran, T. P., *A bibliography of South America* (Buenos Aires, 1912).
Ortega Torres, José Joaquín (b. 1908), *Historia de la literatura colombiana* (Bogotá, 2nd ed., 1935).
Ospina, Joaquín (b. 1875), *Diccionario biográfico y bibliográfico de Colombia* (3 volumes, Bogotá, 1927-35).
Oswald, John Clyde, *Printing in the Americas* (New York, 1937).
Otero Múñez, Gustavo (b. 1894), *Historia de la literatura colombiana* (Bogotá, 3rd ed., 1935).
——, *Semblanzas colombianas* (2 volumes, Bogotá, 1938).

Palau y Dulcet, Antonio (b. 1870), *Manual del librero hispano-americano* (7 volumes, Barcelona, 1923-27).
Pan American Book Shelf (Washington, Pan American Union, March, 1938 ff.).
Parker, William Belmont (b. 1871), *Argentines of today* (2 volumes, New York, 1920).
——, *Bolivians of today* (New York, 1920).
——, *Chileans of today* (New York, 1920).
——, *Cubans of today* (New York, 1919).
——, *Paraguayans of today* (New York, 1921).
——, *Peruvians of today* (New York, Lima, 1919).
——, *Uruguayans of today* (New York, 1921).
Paz y Miño, Luis Telmo (b. 1884), *Bibliografía geográfica ecuatoriana* (Quito, 1929).
Pedreira, Antonio Salvador (1899-1939), *Bibliografía puertorriqueña, 1493-1930* (Madrid, 1932).
Peixoto, Afranio (b. 1876), *Panorama da literatura brasileira* (São Paulo, 1940).

Penney, Clara Louisa, *List of books printed before 1601 in the library of the Hispanic Society of America* (New York, 1929).

——, *List of books printed 1601-1700 in the library of the Hispanic Society of America* (New York, 1938).

Peraza Sarausa, Fermín (ed.), *Anuario bibliográfico cubano* (Habana, 1937).

Pérez, Luis Mariano (b. 1882), *Apuntes de libros y folletos impresos en España y el extranjero que tratan expresamente de Cuba desde principios del siglo XVII hasta 1812 . . .* (Habana, 1907).

Phillips, Philip Lee (1857-1924), *A list of books, magazine articles, and maps relating to Brazil in the Library of Congress . . . 1800-1900* (Washington, 1901).

——, *A list of books, magazine articles, and maps relating to Central America* (Washington, 1902).

——, *A list of books, magazine articles and maps relating to Chile* (Washington, 1903).

Picón-Febres, Gonzalo (1860-1918), *La literatura venezolana en el siglo diez y nueve* (Caracas, 1906).

Picón-Salas, M. (b. 1901), *Formación y proceso de la literatura venezolana* (Caracas, 1941).

Piferrer, Francisco (1813-1863), *Nobiliario de los reinos y señorios de España* (6 volumes, Madrid, 2nd ed., 1857-1860).

Pinart, Alphonse Louis (b. 1852), *Catalogue des livres rares et précieux manuscrits et imprimés principalement sur l'Amérique et sur les langues du monde entier* (Paris, 1883).

Pinto, Juan, *Panorama de la literatura argentina contemporanea* (Buenos Aires, 1941).

Pirotto, Armando D., *La literatura en América: el coloniaje* [to 1767] (Buenos Aires, 1937).

Polo, José Toribio, *Bibliografía geográfica del Perú, siglo XVI* (Lima, 1935).

Posada, Eduardo (b. 1862), *Bibliografía bogotana* (2 volumes, Bogotá, 1917-25).

Prince, Carlos, I. *Bosquejo de la literatura peruana colonial . . .*; II. *Bibliotheca peruana de la colonia . . .* (Lima 1910-1911) and *Suplemento* (Lima, 1912).

——, *Las peruanófilos anticuarios del siglo XIX* (Lima, 1908).

Quaritch, Bernard (1819-1899), *Bibliotheca hispana* (London, 1895).

Raines, Cadwell Walton (1839-1906), *A bibliography of Texas* (Austin, 1934).

Ramírez, José Fernando (1804-1871), *Bibliotheca mexicana . . .* (London, 1880).

Ramos, Roberto, *Bibliografía de la revolución mexicana* (Vol. I, Mexico, 1931).

Reid,——, *Bibliotheca americana* (London, 1789).

Remos y Rubio, Juan N. José (b. 1896), *Resumen de historia de la literatura cubana* (Havana, 1930).

René Moreno, Gabriel (1834-1908), *Biblioteca peruana* (2 volumes, Santiago, Chile, 1896).

——, *Ensayo de una bibliografía general de los periódicos de Bolivia, 1825-1905,* and supplement, 1905-1907 (2 volumes, Santiago, Chile, 1905-07).

Reyles, Carlos (1868-1938), *Historia sintética de la literatura uruguaya* (3 volumes, Montevideo, 1931).

Revista bibliográfica cubana (Havana, 1936 ff.).

Rich, Obadiah (1777-1850), *A catalogue of books relating principally to America arranged under the years in which they were printed* (London, 1832). Books printed between the years 1500 and 1700.

——, *Bibliotheca americana nova.* Vol. I, 1701-1800 (London and New York, 1835).

——, *Bibliotheca americana nova.* Vol. II, 1801-1844 (London, 1846).

Rodrigues, José Carlos (1844-1922), *Bibliotheca brasiliense* (Rio de Janeiro, 1907).

Rojas, Ricardo (b. 1882), *Historia de la literatura argentina* (8 volumes, Buenos Aires, 1924-25).

Rolando, Carlos A., *Obras públicas ecuatorianas* (Guayaquil, 1930).

Roorbach, Orville Augustus (1803-1861), *Biblioteca americana. Catalogue of American publications . . . 1820-1852* (New York, 1852).

Roth, Henry Ling (b. 1855), "Bibliography and cartography of Hispaniola" in Royal Geographical Society, *Supplementary Papers* (London, 1887, Vol. II, p. 41-97).

Roxlo, Carlos (1860-1926), *Historia crítica de la literatura uruguaya* (7 volumes, Montevideo, 1912-16).

Rumazo González, Alfonso (b. 1903), *Historia de la literatura ecuatoriana* (5 volumes, Quito, 1935).

Sabin, J. (1821-1881), *Bibliotheca americana* (29 volumes, New York, 1868-1936).

Salas, Carlos I. (1864-1921), *Bibliografía del general Don José de San Martín y de la emancipación sudamericana* (5 volumes, Buenos Aires, 1910) and supplementary volume by Ricardo Victorica (Buenos Aires, 1912).

Salazar y Roig, Salvador (b. 1892), *Historia de la literatura cubana* (Havana, 1921).

Salvá y Pérez, Vicente (1786-1849), *Catálogo de la biblioteca de Salvá* (2 volumes, Valencia, 1872).

——, A *catalogue of Spanish and Portuguese books with occasional literary and bibliographical remarks* (London, 1826).

Sánchez, Carlos Enríquez, *La imprenta en el Ecuador 1534-1934* (Quito, 1935).

Sánchez, José Rogerio (b. 1876), *Autores españoles e hispano-americanos* (Madrid, 1911).

Sánchez, Luis Alberto (b. 1900), *Historia de la literatura americana* (Santiago, Chile, 1937 and 1940).
——, *Historia de la literatura peruana* (Vol. I, Lima, 1912).
Sánchez, Manuel Segundo, *Bibliografía venezolanista* (Caracas, 1914).
Sánchez Alonzo, B., *Fuentes de la historia española e hispano-americana . . .* (Madrid, 2nd ed., 1927).
Sánchez Garciá, José Rodríguez, *Autores españoles e hispano-americanos . . .* (Madrid, 1911).
Santiago Vela, Gregorio de (1865-1924), *Ensayo de una biblioteca ibero-americano de la orden de San Agustín* (8 volumes, Madrid, 1913-31).
Santos, Manoel dos (bookseller), *Bibliografia geral . . . desde o seculo XV . . .* (Lisbon, 1914-17). Catalogues.
Serrano y Sanz, D., *Historiadores de Indias* (2 volumes, Madrid, 1909).
Silva, Inocencio Francisco de (1810-1876), *Diccionario bibliografico portugues* (23 volumes, Lisbon, 1858-1927).
Silva Castro, Raúl (b. 1903), *Fuentos bibliográficos para el estudio de la literatura chilena* (Santiago, 1933).
Smith, A. R., *Bibliotheca americana. Catalogue of a valuable collection of books and pamphlets illustrating the history and geography of North and South America and the West Indies* (London, 1874).
Sousa, J. C. P. de, *Bibliotheca historica de Portugal a seus dominios ultramerinos* (Lisbon, 1801).
Spain and Spanish America in the libraries of the University of California. A catalogue of books. Vol. I, *The general and departmental libraries* (Berkeley, 1928); Vol. II, *The Bancroft library* (Berkeley, 1930).
Squier, Ephraim George (1821-1888), *Monograph of authors who have written on the languages of Central America . . .* (Albany and New York, 1861).
Stetson, John B. Jr., *Romances of chivalry . . . rare americana* (New York, 1935).
Stevens, Henry (1819-1886), *Bibliotheca historica* (Boston, 1870).
——, *Historical nuggets* (3 volumes, London, 1857-85).
Stillwell, Margaret Bingham (b. 1887), *Incunabula and americana, 1450-1800* (New York, 1931).
Streit, Robert (1875-1930), *Bibliotheca missionum. Americanische missions literatur, 1493-1909* (9 volumes, Münster, 1916-36).
Suárez, Julio, *Catálogo de libros americanos* (2 volumes, Buenos Aires, 1933-35).

Teixidor, Felipe, *Bibliografia yucateca* (Mérida, 1937).
Ternaux-Compans, Henri (1807-1864), *Bibliothèque américaine* (Paris, 1837).
Ticknor, George (1791-1871), *History of Spanish literature* (3 volumes, New York, 1849).
Tiele, Pieter Anton (1834-1889), *Nederlandsche bibliographie van land-en volkenkunden* (Amsterdam, 1884).
Toro, Josefina del, *A bibliography of the collective biography of Spanish America* (Rio Piedras, P. R., 1938).

Torres Rioseco, Arturo (b. 1897), *Antología de la literatura hispanoamericana* (New York, 2nd ed., 1941).
Trelles y Govín, Carlos Manuel (b. 1866), *Ensayo de bibliografía cubana en los siglos XVII y XVIII* (2 volumes, Matanzas, 1907-08).
——, *Bibliografía cubana del siglo XIX* (10 volumes, Matanzas, 1911-17).
——, *Bibliografía cubana del siglo XX* (2 volumes, Matanzas, 1916-17).
——, *Biblioteca científica cubana* (2 volumes, Matanzas, 1918-19).
——, *Biblioteca geográfica cubana* (Matanzas, 1920).
——, *Biblioteca histórica cubana* (3 volumes, Matanzas, 1922-26).
Trömel, Paul, *Bibliothèque américaine* . . . (Leipzig, 1861).
Trübner and Co., *Bibliotheca hispano-americana* (London, 1878).

Udaondo, Enrique, *Diccionario biográfico argentino, [1800-1920]* (Buenos Aires, 1938).

Vaïsse, Emilio (b. 1860), *Bibliografía general de Chile* (2 volumes, Santiago, Chile, 1914-15).
Valdaspe, Tristán, *La historia de la literatura argentina y hispanoamericana* (Buenos Aires, 1937).
Valenzuela, Gilberto, *La imprenta en Guatemala* (Guatemala, 1934).
——, *Bibliografía guatemalteca* . . . (Vol. I, Guatemala, 1933).
Valtón, Emilio, *Impresos mexicanos del siglo XVI* . . . (Mexico, 1935).
Vargas Ugarte, Rubén, *Historia del Perú. Fuentes* (Lima, 1939).
——, *Manuscritos peruanos en las bibliotecas del extranjero* (Lima, 1935 ff.).
Vedia, Enrique de, *Historiadores primitivos de Indias* (2 volumes, Madrid, 1852-53).
Velázquez Bringas, Esperanza (b. 1899), and Rafael Heliodoro Valle (b. 1891), *Indice de escritores* (Mexico, 1928).
Velho Sobrinho, J. F., *Diccionario bio-bibliographico bresileiro* (Vol. I, Rio de Janeiro, 1937).
Vergara y Vergara, José María, *Historia de la literatura en Nueva Granada 1538-1820* (2 volumes, Bogotá, 1931).
Verissimo de Mattos, José (b. 1857), *Estudios de litteratura brasileira* (6 volumes, Rio de Janeiro, 1901-07).
——, *Historia da litteratura brasileira* (Rio de Janeiro, 1903).
Vicuña Mackenna, Benjamín (1831-1886), *Bibliografía americana* . . . (Valparaiso, 1879).
Vilar y Pascual, Luis, *Diccionario histórico, genealógico y heráldico de las familias ilustres de la monarquía española* (8 volumes, Madrid, 1859-66).
Viñaza, Cipriano Múñoz y Manzano, Conde de la (b. 1862), *Bibliografía española de lenguas indígenas de América* (Madrid, 1892).
Vindel, F. (bookseller), *Manuel gráfico-descriptivo del bibliófilo hispano-americano, 1475-1850* (11 volumes in 12, Madrid, 1930-31).

Wagner, Henry Raup (b. 1862), "Sixteenth century Mexican imprints" in *Bibliographical Essays . . .* (Cambridge, 1924).
——, *The Spanish Southwest, 1542-1794. An annotated bibliography* (Berkeley, 1924), revised in 2 volumes (Albuquerque, 1937).
Warden, David Baille (1778-1845), *Bibliotheca americo-septentrionalis . . .* (Paris, 1820).
Whitney, James Lyman (1835-1910), *Catalogue of the Spanish library and the Portuguese books bequeathed by George Ticknor to the Boston Public Library* (Boston, 1879).
Wilgus, A. Curtis (b. 1897), *The Histories of Hispanic America* (Washington, 1932).
—— "Some sixteenth century histories and historians" in *Bulletin* of the Pan American Union (July and September, 1933; April, May and July, 1936; May 1938; January, 1939, May, 1940; March, 1941).

Ximeno, Vicente (d. 1764), *Escritores del Reyno de Valencia . . . 1238 hasta 1747* (2 volumes, Valencia, 1747-49).

Yaben, Jacinto R., *Bibliografías argentinas y sudamericanas* (5 volumes, Buenos Aires, 1938-40).

Zum Felde, Alberto (b. 1888), *La literatura del Uruguay* (Buenos Aires, 1939).

INDEX OF AUTHORS AND EDITORS